Peakland Roads and Trackways

A E Dodd & E M Dodd

Moorland Publishing

British Library Cataloguing in Publication Data

Dodd, Arthur Edward
  Peakland roads and trackways. - 2nd ed.
  1. Roads - England - Peak, The - History
  I. Title II. Dodd, Evelyn Mary
  388.1'09425'11   HE363.G74P/

ISBN 0-86190-004-9

First Edition 1974
Revised and Enlarged Second Edition 1980

ISBN 0 86190 004 9

Typeset by Alacrity Phototypesetters,
Banwell Castle, Weston-super-Mare, Avon
and printed in Great Britain by
Redwood Burn Ltd, Trowbridge and Esher for
Moorland Publishing Co Ltd,
9-11 Station Street, Ashbourne, Derbyshire

PEAKLAND ROADS AND TRACKWAYS

Contents

Preface

Roads are a part of our lives: perhaps for this very reason we take them for granted, accepting the maze of roads and lanes as things primeval, giving no thought as to why a road should alter direction at a particular point, or why one arm of a crossroads should have degenerated into a mere footpath.

To begin to answer such questions requires a map, and for use with this book the map should be the Ordnance Survey Tourist Map of the Peak District: the scale is one inch to the mile and it is marked with the National Grid Reference System. How to use this system is explained on the map itself, and where we give a Grid Reference we have omitted the grid letters as the note on the map suggests. If a reader becomes especially interested in a particular area, the appropriate 2½ in (1:25,000) Ordnance Survey map should be obtained.

Armed with a good map, the next essential is some means of transport and willingness to walk a few miles: with an objective in view, such as signs of some pre-turnpike road, even the 'non-walker' will find that a mile or two on foot is no hardship. Then, having become really interested, we hope that he will set out to discover for himself some of the many trackways, packhorse ways and lengths of turnpike road that we are well aware have inevitably been omitted from this book.

We have attempted to treat roads and trackways chronologically from prehistoric times to the mid-nineteenth century, but this has raised problems; some prehistoric trackways were incorporated in Roman roads, some Roman roads eventually became turnpikes; packhorse ways were also used by ordinary travellers. For such reasons a strict classification of roads and trackways is not possible and the reader will find frequent cross-reference from one chapter to another. He will also see that we have drawn freely from the work of others and we trust that adequate recognition of this is given in the text and bibliography. We have also received much help by way of correspondence and personal contact, as will be seen from the acknowledgements.

And we shall not readily forget the unfailing kindness that we have met with as we have walked along these Peakland ways; so many, whose names we do not know, have given us of their time and knowledge, and we would thank them for those snippets of local history that so often pass unrecorded.

Preface to Second Edition

It would seem that roads and trackways interest more people, both young and old, than we had realized when the First Edition of this book was published six years ago. That edition became out-of-print more rapidly than was expected. However, we had already started to amass further information and to carry out additional field-work — rather for our own satisfaction than in anticipation of a demand for a further edition. We are grateful to the Moorland Publishing Company for their decision to embark on this Second Edition, and we have grasped the opportunity to offer readers what we believe to be a much more comprehensive book. The few errors in the original edition to which our attention was drawn have been corrected and, perhaps of greater overall importance, we have acquired and, we trust, passed on, a clearer picture of the evolution of a network of trackways into the system of turnpikes that are now our motor-roads.

Comparison of the two editions will also reveal some re-arrangements. Although the packhorse ways, salt-ways and drovers' roads — the Trade Routes of the First Edition — mostly developed from the Middle Ages, it has now seemed more logical for the first four chapters to follow the story of roads from prehistory through the Roman occupation to the Saxons with their portways, continuing through the Middle Ages, directly into Tudor and Stuart times — the beginning of the modern age of 'Travel for All'. The subsequent more detailed consideration of packhorse ways then leads in to the turnpike era.

In the Dark and Middle Ages chapter we have been able to add a section on the intriguing *Via de Peco* — 'Peakway'. As yet, only a short length of this ancient way to the Peak can be identified; perhaps some lover of the Peak District will become sufficiently fascinated by this problematic route to wish to search out its course over a longer distance. Other gaps in our knowledge will become evident to the careful reader; from our own happy experience over many years we can assure anyone who feels attracted to the task of filling some of these gaps that the time spent — now in some library amongst archives and now tramping some breezy moorland — will prove both enjoyable and rewarding.

1 Prehistoric Trackways

What would the world be, once bereft
Of wet and of wildness? Let them be left,
O let them be left, wildness and wet;
Long live the weeds and the wilderness yet.

Gerard Manley Hopkins

Primeval wildness and wet can still be found on the high moors of the northernmost areas of the Peak District; Bleaklow and Kinderscout may be more wild now than in prehistoric times, for souring by spreading peat has forced the tree line further into the valleys. Elsewhere in the Peak District, when the first hunters of the Old Stone Age, or Palaeolithic Period, penetrated into these hills they would find vast forests and, being hunters, would follow in any direction the animals that provided their food and clothing. In Britain the Palaeolithic Period lasted from some indefinitely remote past until about 5,000 BC, when improved tools and weapons were introduced by the Middle Stone Age peoples; this Mesolithic Period was relatively short, lasting only from about 5,000 BC to 3,000 BC. The Mesolithic peoples, still nomadic hunters, made much use of the black Derbyshire chert, a hard rock found along the Wye valley between Buxton and Bakewell. These primitive wanderers over our then wooded hills moved over considerable distances; their rough, but hard, chert weapons have been found in Longdendale, on the moors west of Huddersfield, and even as far away as Alderley Edge in Cheshire.

With the arrival from Europe of people of the New Stone Age, or Neolithic Period, in about 3,000 BC, there came a profound change. The Neolithic peoples were farmers rather than huntsmen; they kept herds and grew a primitive type of wheat, and so they needed clearings in the forests where their herds could graze, arable strips for their wheat and, for themselves, permanent huts for shelter. These Neolithic farmers cleared forests quite extensively; many of the polished stone axe-heads that they used have been found in the Peak District and careful study of the fine-grained igneous rock from which these axe-heads were almost invariably made has shown that, for the most part, they came from Great Langdale in the Lake District. The site of the Langdale 'axe factory' is known, and there must have been trade routes from there into the Peak District and into many other parts of England. These trade routes would

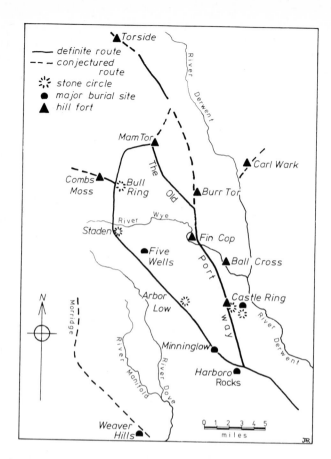

Map 1 Prehistoric trackways in the Peak District.

Legend:
— definite route
--- conjectured route
stone circle
● major burial site
▲ hill fort

follow, as far as possible, well-drained ridges — they would be 'ridge-ways' and would require very little constructional work except where they had to cross a valley.

1.1 Trackways to the Henges

Equipped with their Langdale axes, the Neolithic farmers first cleared the limestone uplands; these were, and still are, well-drained and more easily cultivated than the peaty gritstone country. The most extensive limestone upland in the Peak District lies between the rivers Derwent and Dove, and it is fairly certain that there was a Neolithic trackway running roughly north-south along this limestone plateau on which, at Arbor Low (161636) is the third largest henge, or stone circle, in England; like Stonehenge, it is a monument, presumably built for religious purposes, of the Late Neolithic or Early Bronze Age, dating from around 2,000 BC. Rather more than 300yd south-west of Arbor Low there is an oval barrow known as Gib Hill and adjacent to this barrow, on the north-west, is an almost obliterated circular earthwork that recent excavation has suggested to be the remains of a henge still older than Arbor Low. This would account for the prehistoric trackway bypassing Arbor Low by some 500yd; the trackway must have pre-dated Arbor Low for it passes much closer to the original henge near Gib Hill.

Another curious feature of Arbor Low is the 'earthwork' that curves from the south-west towards one of its entrances. Its purpose has never been decided, but from this recent observation of the site of an earlier henge close to the prehistoric trackway (which the Romans later improved to make their Street, p27), one may deduce that the embankment was an approach way from the trackway to the henge. The older henge had been demolished and a larger one had been built in a more imposing position but some distance from the 'Pilgrims' Way'; what could be more natural than to complete the work by constructing an approach from the trackway to the new henge?

There are further features to support the view that this trackway, which we now rightly call a Roman road, existed when Arbor Low was a place of pilgrimage. If we follow this straight track for five miles south-east over Smerrill Moor, we come to Minninglow (209572), a prehistoric cemetery, and not far away are Stony Low and Green Low, other burial sites. If continued for a further 2½ miles, this south-east line passes very near to Harboro Rocks (243554) where there is yet another of these prehistoric burial places. Proceeding in the opposite direction from Arbor Low along this ancient trackway that later became the

Map 2 Arbor Low and its associated trackways.

11

Roman road, we pass the henge at Staden (069721) and then the Bull Ring (078783); this lies east of Dove Holes cricket ground and is best approached from a point on the A6 opposite Dove Holes post office. It was once a henge similar to Arbor Low but has long since been robbed of its stones. Walking on these uplands, especially on a day of mist, we need but little imagination to picture groups of roughly clad people coming from afar, north and south, to one or other of the immemorial shrines that stood beside one of the oldest trackways in Britain.

In the fifth century BC bronze was being replaced as a metal for tools and weapons by the harder, but more difficultly smelted, iron. In Britain, this transition was at first confined to the south-east lowlands; in the more remote Peak District, the older Bronze Age culture for long persisted. The most conspicuous Iron Age features in our upland areas are the hillforts, such as that on Mam Tor (128836). This particular Iron Age fort, the largest in the Peak District, was built in a position dominating the still older trackway running along Rushup Edge, over Lord's Seat with its Bronze Age burial mound, and then high on the northern flank of Mam Tor itself; there are traces of a hollow-way slanting up the hill to the well-guarded south-west entrance to the fort. Today, at least 3,000 years after men first travelled along it, this ridgeway still makes one of the finest hill walks in the Peak District, with continuously grand views to the north across the Vale of Edale to Kinderscout and Edale Moor. The destination of this prehistoric trackway beyond Lose Hill (153853) is by no means clear, but in the opposite direction an extension of Rushup Edge bears off south-west and the trackway may well have run down this shoulder to the Bull Ring henge. More likely, for the greater convenience of pilgrims, the henge was sited at the junction of three pre-existing trackways — one coming from Arbor Low to the south, a second coming from the east along Rushup Edge, with a third trackway leading in from the west.

1   Hollins Cross on the ridgeway between Mam Tor and Lose Hill.

This surmised western way could have passed through what is now Cheshire, and so have led to a sea route to Ireland; many of the bronze tools and weapons that have given the Bronze Age its name were probably imported from Ireland, so there must have been some trade route linking that country with the Peak District where many Bronze Age artifacts have been found. Support for the existence of such a route is the Iron Age fort on the north-west of Combs Moss (054785), a position well chosen if the Iron Age invaders wished to control a major line of communication of the Bronze Age folk whom they were bent on dominating. A trackway can be followed on the north-east flank of the precipitous hill on which Combs Moss fort stands, but its true age is difficult to assess; the hollow-way that makes a hairpin bend to come into the fort by its original northern entrance and then leaves by its later central entrance onto the open moor, may be a medieval packhorse way.

1.2 The Old Portway

There is in the Peak District an ancient trackway which for many centuries has been known as the Portway. This is an Old English word for an important highway and will be discussed in more detail in Chapter 3; suffice it to say here that the Anglo-Saxon invaders applied this word of theirs to parts of a trackway through the Peak District that existed many centuries before their arrival. It should therefore be stressed that when tracing this or indeed any other ancient way, one must bear in mind that some lengths of the route may have been used in medieval or still more recent times, that there may have been later diversions from the original prehistoric high-level route, and that the same trackway may have acquired different names at different periods.

The prehistoric way may have crossed the River Derwent near Milford (351451), where there was an ancient ford. From the west bank rises the Chevin, a corruption of the Celtic *cefn* (pronounced with a hard c), meaning ridge. Prehistoric traders would wish to rise clear of the swampy and densely forested valley bottom as quickly as possible; their trackway climbed from the ford through fields behind Moscow Farm and so over the Chevin, before descending to Blackbrook (333478). From there the route was by Longwalls Lane, straight up the opposite hillside; it must then have veered more to the north-west to pass over Alport Hill (305516); note the suffix 'port' relating the hill to the Portway.

At Wirksworth the old way would appear to have changed direction, leading almost due west to Gallows Knoll (266545). From there, having avoided the deep valleys in the neighbourhood of Middleton, the north-west course was resumed along what is known as the Chariot Way. This

Map 3   The southern length of the Old Portway.

2   The Old Portway passes by this rock outcrop on Alport Hill; the guidestone is of much later date than the trackway.

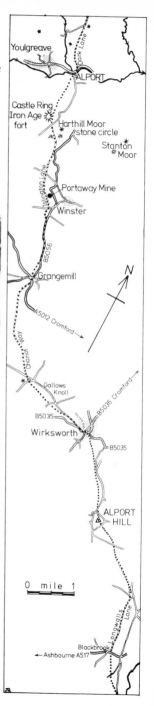

3   The Chariot Way (part of the Old Portway) south of Grangemill.

is the ancient trackway over the hills leading to Grangemill (244576). Access to it can be gained, on foot, by first following a bridleway from a point (252546) about 1½ miles east of Brassington; where the track to the Upper Golconda Mine turns west, continue north along the east side of the wall. A large field here is known as Chariot Field and the Chariot Way soon comes in from the right. That it is an ancient way will be evident; for a short distance it has been metalled to serve a farm, but elsewhere it is for the most part a broad green lane.

The prehistoric trackway seems to have descended to Grangemill and then to have continued north along the general line of the present road to Winster as far as Bonsall Lane, coming in from the east; about 100yd further along the Winster road, a by-road forks left and soon reaches a minor crossroads — the Old Portway follows the lane ahead, now known as Islington Lane.

This old way crosses the Winster to Elton road and then descends steeply, almost joining the B5056 before rising again to peter out as a footpath between Cratcliff Rocks and Robin Hood's Stride. We may assume that the trackway would pass close to the Harthill Moor Stone Circle (226626), and we may further assume that, during the Iron Age, the hillfort known as Castle Ring (221628) was constructed to dominate this length of the trackway. We are in an area that was populous a thousand years before the Iron Age people threw up Castle Ring; on Stanton Moor, east of the B5056, there is another stone circle and a large number of Bronze Age burial mounds, in one of which was found a glass bead of a type that could only, at that remote period, have come from Egypt. Evidently, 3,500 years ago, there was trade between the eastern Mediterranean and Britain, and foreign luxury goods were being carried from ancient sea-ports along old trackways such as this, even as far inland as the Peak District.

A good mile north of Castle Ring, at the point where the River Bradford joins the Lathkill, is the picturesque hamlet of Alport; it stands at the site of an ancient ford. The prehistoric way continued north up Dark Lane which soon reaches unspoiled country and becomes a footpath beside the western boundary wall of Haddon Fields to join the Youlgreave to Bakewell road at a point (216662) close to a tumulus. The way continued along the flank of Burton Moor, above Bakewell, to ford the River Wye at Ashford.

As we climb north from Ashford, a great hill promontory commanding Monsal Dale lies on our left; it is crowned by an Iron Age fort with the striking name of Fin Cop (175709) and this stronghold would control the trackway as it crossed open land 400ft below. The line of the old way is followed closely by the present B6465 to the fine viewpoint at Monsal Head, on past Rolley Low (183736) to Wardlow (181747). Beyond that

4 The Old Portway, now Islington Lane, near Winster.

5 The Old Portway forded the River Lathkill near this bridge at Alport.

Map 4 The northern length of the Old Portway.

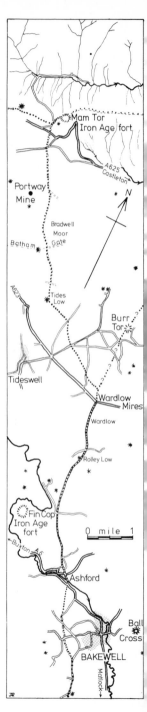

6   The Old Portway
crossed the River Wye
by a ford at Ashford.

village, however, the Old Portway may have divided, one branch continuing due north while the other moved off north-west.

The conjecture that one prehistoric trackway maintained the same
general direction as that followed from Monsal Head, is based on the
need, during the Iron Age, to link one fort with another — in this case the
fort on Fin Cop with that at Burr Tor (178786). From Burr Tor this
branch of the Old Portway is likely to have been the ridgeway along the
western scarp of Abney Moor, over Bleak Knoll (183798) and Bradwell
Edge (182805), coming down again at Brough; beyond there, the prehistoric trackway may have coincided with Doctor's Gate (p38) as far
as the Woodlands Valley, before continuing north above Alport Dale,
over Alport Moor (120937) to the ancient earthworks at Torside
(077965).

The more well-defined branch of the Old Portway turned north-west
beyond Wardlow Mires (181756); the line is followed by the Tideswell
parish boundary, crossing the Tideswell to Bradwell road at Benstor
House (164769) and continuing up the fields to meet the next lane near
Poyntoncross Barn (160777); here, the parish boundary follows the lane
but the Old Portway aimed for Tides Low — the hilltop tumulus
(150779) not Tideslow Farm. This tumulus is the largest in the Peak District; when excavated it was found to contain a single standing stone
showing no structural connection with the complex of stone burial cists.
Did this standing stone pre-date the tumulus? If so, it may well have been
erected as a landmark on the prehistoric trackway which here changes
direction, the more northerly line being taken up by a broad, but un-
tarmac'd lane (also a parish boundary) that crosses the Roman road
(p33). The lane peters out in an old lead-mining area, important because
one of the mines was known as Portway Mine (128810), thus confirming
the route which we have been following. The line continues as a
footpath over Bradwell Moor at 1,518ft, and Old Moor at about 1,400

feet. Beyond a meeting-of-the-ways a more pronounced track takes us west of Rowtor Farm and we can now see where this branch of the Old Portway was heading for — the great Iron Age fort on Mam Tor (128837).

1.3 Other Prehistoric Trackways

If we look at the map (p10) of prehistoric trackways in the Peak District we will see how well the main routes linked the henge monuments and, later, the Iron Age hillforts. However, the forts at Ball Cross (228691) on the high ground east of Bakewell, and at Carl Wark (260815) two miles east of Hathersage, remain unaccounted for. It is possible that the somewhat isolated Ball Cross fort, which has only one bank and ditch and covers less than two acres, was the stronghold of some Iron Age chieftain who was lord of the high ground between the Wye and the Derwent; it is not comparable in importance to Fin Cop, Mam Tor, Combs Moss or Burr Tor which all give the impression of having been sited to dominate lines of communication.

The promontory fort at Carl Wark, although covering an area little greater than Ball Cross, has been described as 'among the most spectacular and easily accessible in this country' — easily accessible, that is, in the absence of early-British warriors! Whether the Carl Wark warriors were of the Iron Age or the Dark Age (immediately post-Roman) is still a subject for debate. So, too, is the line of communication to this hillfort although, quite recently, traces have been reported of a Roman road (p38) passing nearby.

Lastly, on Map 1, there is the ridgeway that follows the high curve of Morridge, near Leek. The south-west boundary of the Peak Park and a good road both follow this ridgeway for several miles; on a clear day the view extends to the Berwyns in North Wales. There is no direct evidence that this ridgeway is prehistoric, but if we are prepared to link the Morridge ridgeway via the old landmark known as Waterfall Cross to the Weaver Hills (100460) it would have provided a line of communication in the Bronze Age for the folk who buried their dead on those hills. Continuous high ground would provide linking ridges to the prehistoric trackways around Buxton and Chapel en le Frith.

2 Roman Roads

*Now the straight line to Rome ran from where I
stood . . . and this mixture of roads and paths
I exactly followed, so as to march on as directly
as possible towards Rome, which was my goal.*

Hilaire Belloc   *The Path to Rome*

We all know that Julius Caesar landed on the south coast of Britain in
55 BC and again in 54 BC, but we should remember that these landings
were little more than reconnaissances; most of another century elapsed
before the Roman legions came to stay, this time for 350 years. The
south-east of Britain was subdued relatively quickly and a frontier was
established in 47 AD on a line running roughly from the Severn estuary
to north of the Wash; this line was protected by a series of forts, linked at
a later date by a military road — the Fosse Way. London was connected
with the Fosse Way at about its mid-point by Watling Street; other
roads were built from London to Cirencester in the south-west and from
London to Lincoln in the north-east.

Before they advanced further, the Romans foresaw the necessity to
protect their western flank against the warlike Silures in what is now
South Wales. To achieve this, they pushed across the Severn and constructed forts linked by a military road running northwards from Cirencester, at the same time extending Watling Street westwards from its
junction with the Fosse Way; where the two roads met, near what is
now Shrewsbury, they built an important fortified town — Viroconium. With this protection, the Romans left the Silures for the time
being to their own devices while the legions attacked the Ordovices in
Central and North Wales, with a view to a subsequent campaign against
the Brigantes north of the Trent. The Ordovices were defeated in
AD 51; Caratacus, their leader, fled to Cartimandua, Queen of the
Brigantes, who tried to preserve her own tribe by handing him over to
the Romans. This act of treachery led to civil war north of the Trent and
for the next few years the Romans were content to watch the powerful
Brigantes weaken themselves by internecine strife.

In AD 59 Suetonius Paullinus took command of Britain and, two years
later, subdued Anglesey; this campaign necessitated a seaport at Chester
and a further extension of Watling Street from Viroconium to Chester.

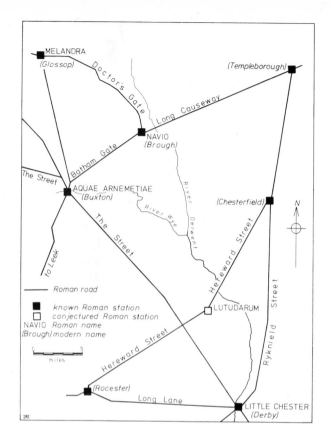

Map 5   Roman roads in the Peak District (diagrammatic).

By this time, also, Ryknield Street, coming up from the direction of Cirencester to join Watling Street at Wall (near Lichfield) had probably been advanced from there to a fort on the west bank of the Derwent in what is now Strutt's Park, Derby. This fort would seem to have been occupied until about 80 AD when Little Chester was established on the other side of the river. In passing, we might note that the Roman name for their fort at Little Chester was Derventio, taken from the ancient Celtic name of the river — Derwent — on which it stood.

The lines of communication were now complete for a pincer movement on the Brigantes, north of the Trent, but while Paullinus was in Wales, Boudica, Queen of the Iceni in what is now East Anglia, led a rebellion in which London, St Albans and Colchester were devastated and their inhabitants slaughtered. This delayed progress of the Roman conquest of Britain for ten years; it was not until AD 71 that the legions again pushed forward to establish a fort at York. Prior to this northern advance, a road was built from Little Chester near Derby westwards through Rocester and Chesterton near Newcastle under Lyme to the

Mersey; later, in AD 78-84 when Agricola was Governor of Britain, Roman forts were set up at Templeborough (Sheffield), Brough (182-827), Glossop and Manchester with roads connecting them. Behind this advanced frontier with the Brigantes, roads linked Little Chester to Buxton and Manchester, Little Chester via Chesterfield to Templeborough, and Buxton to Brough and also to Glossop. With his bases in the south secure and with this elaborate system of supply and support routes, Agricola now swept forward and, by AD 80, had overrun all northern England and was securing his frontier with Scotland.

This, then, is the background of the slow Roman advance from lowland Britain into, and beyond, the less easily subdued uplands of the Peak District. Behind the legions excellent roads ran back to the centre of administration in Rome itself. When the Roman Empire was at its zenith, its network of communications included 180,000 miles of paved roads, nearly a third of this vast mileage being major highways up to 40ft wide. These primarily served the Cursus Publicus, or State Mail Service, which also provided transport for state officials. Express messengers could travel up to 150 miles in a day, but Roman government officials would not exceed forty to fifty miles in a day. On major roads, posting stations (*mutationes*) were provided for changing horses at intervals of about eight miles with rest-houses (*mansiones*) every twenty to twenty-five miles for overnight stops.

The Roman roads in the Peak District were not major highways; in fact most of the Roman roads in Britain were no more than 16ft wide. They were nevertheless well constructed. Where drainage was necessary, as in the more peaty areas of the Dark Peak, ditches were first dug on both sides, the space between being excavated to a firm foundation on which large rough stones were laid, these being then covered with finer material; some lengths of road were fully paved. Roman roads, as we all know, almost invariably proceeded in a series of straight lines, sometimes continuing for many miles before making a relatively small change in direction; but as we have already seen, if the terrain was suitable, the pre-Roman trackways were also straight — even primitive peoples well knew that the shortest distance between two points is a straight line.

2.1 Long Lane

The road connecting the Roman station at Little Chester (355376), near Derby, with Rocester (110393), just over the border in Staffordshire, lies outside the Peak District and will therefore not be dealt with in detail. For the first three miles west of Little Chester there is little trace of this road. The best way to pick up the line is to follow the A52 out of Derby as

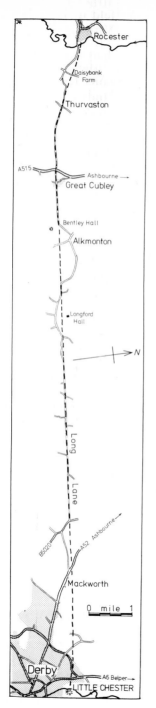

Map 6 (*left*) Long Lane.

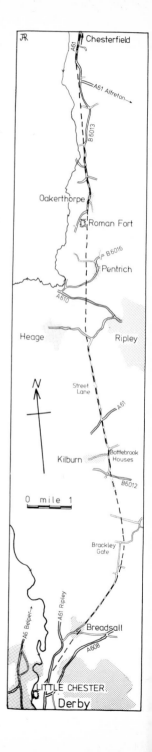

Map 7 (*right*) Ryknield Street.

far as Mackworth and then take the first lane on the left; after about 1½ miles you will be on Long Lane (290380) which runs due west. The present road bends slightly south round the parkland of Longford Hall and then wanders somewhat to the north to pass through Alkmonton, but the Roman road went straight through Longford Park and on through what are now fields where some sections can be traced. The present road rejoins the straight Roman line at Bentley Hall (178381); the name 'Bentley' may refer to the bend away from the original straight Roman road — some other Bentleys are similarly located but many more are not. The present road from Bentley Hall through Great Cubley and across the A515 continues the line of Long Lane for three miles or so to Thurvaston (138585); the original Roman line then passed close to Daisybank Farm (126389) to a crossing of the River Dove near to the present road bridge and so into the Roman station at Rocester by its east gate.

2.2 Ryknield Street

The original Ryknield Street came into Little Chester from Wall; its line is followed very closely by the modern A38. As we have already mentioned, when the legions pushed further north, they extended Ryknield Street through Chesterfield to Templeborough. This road, like Long Lane, lies outside our true boundary, but anyone approaching the southern half of the Peak District from the east, must at some point cross this length of Ryknield Street, so we will follow it as far as Chesterfield.

The route from Little Chester seems to have been through Breadsall (370398); the line is through the fields somewhat to the east of the present road leading to Brackley Gate (388428) where there was a change in direction to very nearly due north. Excavations have shown that the road was about 18 ft wide. The line of the road can be seen hereabouts in the fields and then, as we descend to Bottlebrook Houses (388459), we are on Street Lane (a name which confirms that we are indeed on the line of the Roman *strata*) and this takes us through the hamlet of Street Lane and on as far as a point just short of its junction with the Heage to Ripley road. Here was another small change in direction to a line that brought the road a little to the west of the village of Pentrich and close to, but not actually through, the small Roman fort there (386541); this minor fort must have been thrown up by the Romans at an early date and abandoned before this northern extension of Ryknield Street was constructed.

The Roman road joins B6013 just short of Oakerthorpe (389549). From there the present road through Clay Cross to Chesterfield follows Ryknield Street fairly closely; the village of Stretton (393612) was named from its location on this Street, and the town of Chesterfield was surely so named from its origin as a Roman *castrum*, although it is only recently that a Roman site has been confirmed by excavation.

2.3 Hereward Street

From place-name evidence it would seem that a road linked the Roman station at Rocester with the Roman fort at Chesterfield. This road does not appear to have been recognized as Roman until 1960, when a valuable article on the subject was written by R. W. P. Cockerton, who discovered that, over much of its length, the Rocester to Chesterfield route at one time bore the distinctive name of Hereward Street.

The Romans evidently built their small military station at Rocester to safeguard the crossing of the River Dove. There was already an Iron Age fort at Barrow Hill (112409) rather less than a mile to the north; the Romans presumably overran this tribal stronghold and may later have used it themselves, for Roman pottery and coins have been found there. A deep hollow-way runs from Barrow Hill in the general direction of Ellastone, where we find Dove Street, but whether this is a folk memory of a Roman Street is doubtful. Between Ellastone and Mayfield, on the high ground above Calwich Abbey, the modern road (B5032) passes close to three tumuli half a mile apart and exactly in line, which suggests that the Romans, as so frequently, may have improved a pre-existing trackway.

Before arriving at Mayfield, the road passes through Wallash; the 'Wall' element in this name possibly refers to nearness to a Roman road. The River Dove is crossed at Hanging Bridge, and a document of 1330 referring to land in this area mentions 'Herwardstrete'. Just where the Street ran is uncertain; the present road from Hanging Bridge into Ashbourne is for most of its length a new line cut in turnpike times. It would seem most likely that, once across the River Dove (probably by a ford) the Roman road builders would wish to get clear of the frequently flooded valley bottom as quickly as possible; this they could have achieved by aiming straight through Buckholme (165460) to the ridge that runs north of Ashbourne along Windmill Lane; this ridge road was at one time known as Evenlode — 'the level way'. Windmill Lane runs into the B5035 to Wirksworth and soon brings us to Kniveton where, in the time of Henry III, the road was known as 'Arwey', and in the following reign as 'Harewey'; both these names are related to 'Hereward'. Beyond Kniveton the road climbs Hognaston Winn, where traces of an old road have been found; then in another mile, at White House (234524), the Wirksworth road makes a sharp right-hand turn and we have arrived at a very interesting point. The area north-west of the present road junction is known as 'Wall Lands', strongly suggestive

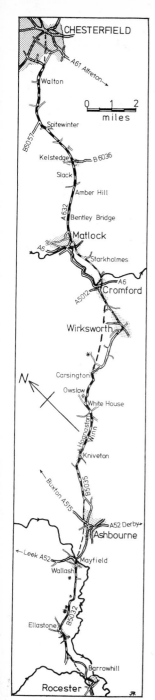

7 Hereward Street crossed the River Dove near Hanging Bridge; the present single arch was built over the two arches of the narrow medieval bridge in 1937.

Map 8 Hereward Street.

The labels on the map read:

CHESTERFIELD
A61 Alfreton
Walton
0 1 2 miles
B5057
Spitewinter
Kelstedge
B6036
Slack
Amber Hill
A632
Bentley Bridge
Matlock
A6
Starkholmes
A5012
A6
Cromford
Wirksworth
Carsington
Owslow
White House
Hognaston Winn
Kniveton
Buxton A515
B5035
A52 Derby
Ashbourne
Leek A52
Mayfield
Wallash
B5032
Ellastone
Barrowhill
Rocester
N

of a Roman presence. To the north-east is Ows Low (238528), a prehistoric burial mound; in a field south-west of the road junction is a standing stone known as 'The Stoup'. In 1946, in one of the fields here, Roman pottery and a Roman pig of lead were unearthed.

Beyond the White House, Hereward Street continued its general north-east direction. It is likely that the Roman lead-mining centre Lutudarum was located in the neighbourhood where pigs of lead bearing the abbreviation 'LUT' have been found. In former days there was a tradition in Wirksworth that the nearby village of Middleton had been a penal settlement for Roman convicts condemned to work in the lead mines; as we shall see later, there was a similar tradition at Brough relating to Bradwell. Perhaps Lutudarum was near Middleton? Quite recently (1975) two more Roman pigs of lead have been unearthed in a field (185399) near Yeaveley; the inscriptions on these pigs have been translated 'Product of the Lutudarum partners: British [lead] from the lead-silver works'.

Until site-evidence is forthcoming to locate this enigmatic Lutudarum elsewhere, circumstantial evidence would seem to support a site on the high ground within a half-mile radius of Middleton Cross; but all this ground has been so much disturbed by mining and quarrying that, even if this surmise is correct, there is little likelihood that any trace of a Roman settlement can have survived. The Middleton Cross area would have been well-placed for supervision of the lead miners and for the control of this length of Hereward Street, which would here seem to have changed direction to descend to a crossing of the Derwent. Cromford is known to have been a ford in Saxon days, and in 1919 a Roman pig of lead was found in Cromford churchyard.

There was no way up the Matlock gorge until about 200 years ago and the route from Cromford would have been up the steep hill through Starkholmes (301587), past Matlock parish church and then in the general direction of the present road (A632) to Chesterfield. At Bentley Bridge (312613) there is a bend — a further example of the place-name 'Bentley' at a bend in an ancient road. Hereward Street then ascends Amber Hill before twisting to ease the gradient of the steep descent through Slack to the crossing of the upper Amber Valley and the village of Kelstedge. Climbing out of the valley, in two more miles the Chesterfield road attains its highest point, 1,043ft, at Spitewinter (341665); R. W. P. Cockerton has traced further early documentary evidence of the name Hereward Street in this area. At Chesterfield, Hereward Street merged into the more important Ryknield Street but, even so, the name persisted further north; in the southern suburbs of Sheffield there is still a Hereward's Road, and this is an old name for it was recorded in the 1815 Enclosure Award for that area.

2.4 The Street

From very early times the Roman road from Little Chester to Buxton has been known as 'The Street'; the first documentary use of this name so far traced was in the year 1415, but the writer of that document evidently assumed that anyone knowing the area would also know where The Street ran. James Pilkington, in his book on Derbyshire written in 1789, appears to have been the first modern writer to recognise this road as Roman: he had no difficulty in tracing the road in the reverse direction from Buxton as far as Pikehall (192592) because it was still in use, but he believed that it then changed its course to aim at a supposed Roman station at Lombard's Green (187555) where Roman coins had been found only a few years before his book was written. We now know that his conjecture was wrong, but the precise course of the southern end of The Street is still uncertain.

There can be no doubt that this Roman road started at Little Chester in the northern suburbs of Derby. The present consensus of opinion is that the River Derwent was crossed immediately opposite the fort, the road then turning sharply to the north. Traces have been observed at several points between Allestree and Kirk Ireton, and the line joining these points passes through Windley (305452) where a fifteenth-century deed mentions 'Le Strete'. It has to be noted, however, that some two miles east of this Windley-Kirk Ireton line there was a 'Street Close' at Blackbrook (333478), where Longwalls Lane has for long been considered Roman. Perhaps it formed part of a branch road related to the Roman kilns at Hazelwood?

Accepting, as one must, the virtually straight line from Little Chester, north-west of Kirk Ireton The Street crossed the Scow Brook and passed through Carsington; by the brook there is a field known as Brough Meadow (252523) and Roman pantiles have been unearthed in the same area (249517). Also, in the eighteenth century, a section of paved road was excavated in the parkland of Hopton Hall. This general line through Carsington leads directly into a length of Roman road recently identified by Wroe and Mellor north of Brassington (237548-229556), where there is also a confirmatory field-name, Straight Knolls (224562) which, in 1620, was 'Streete-Knowle'. The line then leads into the well-known section of The Street near Minninglow.

From Brassington the Roman road near Minninglow can be approached by way of Gallowlow Lane. Just below Minninglow on the north-east is the prehistoric trackway (p11) linking this Bronze Age burial site with Arbor Low and the Bull Ring; the trackway traversed a dry limestone plateau and probably required little modification by the Romans to bring it up to the standard demanded by their minor roads. Excava-

Map 9   (*left*) The middle length of The Street.

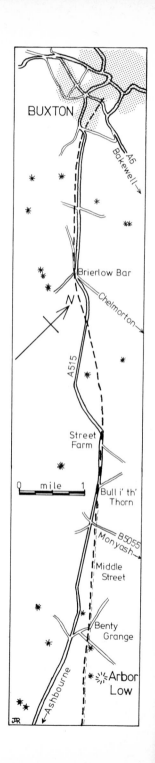

Map 10   (*right*) The northern length of The Street.

tions at Minninglow have turned up Roman pottery and coins, proving disturbance of this Bronze Age site as long ago as the third or fourth century AD.

From Minninglow, The Street forms a parish boundary; for some distance its line can be followed fairly closely by walking along the High Peak Trail. Where this old railway turns sharply south-west to avoid the hill at Gotham, a return to the actual line of The Street (and to the parish boundary) can be made by following Hedge Lane to the Cromford to Newhaven road (A5012). Here is Pikehall, referred to in a document dated 1313 and an inn at least as early as 1675; it was well placed, for Pikehall is a focus of ancient ways and one wonders whether the inn might have stood on the site of a Roman posting house (*mutatio*) — the distance from Roman Buxton would have required a change of horses hereabouts along The Street. From the yard of Pikehall Farm, The Street continued north-north-west up the hill through what is now a narrow plantation and then followed a wall before serving as another parish boundary, making a straight course to Smerrill Barn (184602). Beyond the Newhaven to Youlgreave road (A524) the line of the Roman road is marked for over two miles by a succession of narrow plantations between walls; as these walls are some 50ft apart they probably mark the notional width of the original Derby to Buxton coach road (p76) which followed the Roman and prehistoric line.

Beyond Benty Grange (149642) The Street converges on the modern Ashbourne-Buxton road (A515), passing Middle Street Farm (140651), crossing the Monyash road and ultimately coinciding with the A515 close to the Bull i' th' Thorn Inn (128665). Traces of an old road have been found on the *west* of the A515 in the vicinity of the seventh milestone from Buxton, but there is no clear reason why the Romans should have departed from the straight line through Middle Street which is the generally accepted line of their road.

The motorist travelling to Buxton from the Bull i' th' Thorn drives on The Street for the next mile — as far as Street Farm (118674) and Pomeroy Cottages. On the 1 in OS Map, only Street House is marked; this stands about 300 yd west of the road whereas Street Farm is by the roadside. Beyond Street Farm the A515 veers west past Greatlow, but The Street keeps straight ahead, its line marked by a wall. The boundary between the parish of Hartington and the townships of Chelmorton and Flagg also follows this wall, but then moves sharply north and this can provide a salutary warning that a present-day parish boundary may not be along the line laid down when the parish was formed, perhaps a thousand years ago. This boundary between Hartington on our left and Chelmorton and Flagg on our right, was fixed only in 1799, immediately prior to the Hartington Enclosure Award. The precise line of this boundary had for long been in dispute; arbitration resulted in a compromise between the rival claims, but, if one may judge the question without having to placate contending parishioners, it would seem that the boundary claimed by Chelmorton and Flagg was probably the older, being based on the line of the Roman road. Their claim was for a boundary continuing straight ahead north-west from Street Farm, linking the straight line of The Street from the Bull i' th' Thorn to the straight line 2½ miles further north-west beyond Brierlow Bar (086698) in a very direct manner. In detail, the boundary claimed by Chelmorton and Flagg (where there is a field known as Over Street) continued straight ahead from Street Farm to Blinder House on the lane leading to Chelmorton Thorn (119697), and continued forward where the present (1799 compromise) boundary turns north, then bending slightly and running parallel to the present boundary to cross the A515 near Brierlow Farm (096691); from that point, the boundary claimed by Chelmorton and Flagg ran fairly straight to Brierlow Bar.

The old road — and The Street — from Brierlow Bar was the one that now leads to Harpur Hill. However, where after half a mile the Harpur Hill road veers more to the west, The Street kept straight on, parallel to the A515 and a field's width west. At a point about a mile short of Buxton, a section across the Roman road was cut by Wroe and Mellor while building work was in progress in 1974; they found the original embankment (*agger*) of brown sandy clay with a heavy limestone kerb.

2.5 Aquae Arnemetiae and a road to the south-west

Buxton would attract the Romans because its warm springs permitted them to construct baths, thus bringing some semblance of home to legionaries quartered in our inhospitable hills. The remains of the Roman baths were discovered when excavations were in progress for the foundations of the Crescent, completed in 1796 but, more than two centuries earlier, Dr John Jones mentioned 'vayne invencions about St. Ann found in the Well'. This is believed to have referred to the discovery of a Roman Statue and, if it was indeed found by the hot spring that fed the Roman baths, it is likely to have represented the goddess of the spring, a Celtic goddess whose name the Romans latinized to Arnemetia, giving their settlement its name, Aquae Arnemetiae. It has been plausibly conjectured that the inscription on the statue had become illegible except for the first three letters and that even these were misread as Ann, so that the spring has ever since been known as St Ann's Well.

The Roman station itself stood on high ground in what is now Higher Buxton. In 1856 a Roman milestone was dug up in a garden in Silverlands near the old Upper Buxton Railway Station; it is preserved in Buxton Museum and the inscription shows that it stood eleven Roman miles from Navio, the Roman fort at Brough. Some sixty years ago there were still traces of the Roman road as it descended by a made terrace from the neighbourhood of the milestone to a crossing of the River Wye near the railway viaduct. About a mile and a half north of Buxton the Roman road forked, Batham Gate (p33) leading to Navio, and an unnamed road (p42) leading to Melandra.

The route taken by the Roman road leading from Buxton to the south-west is generally considered to have followed the series of straight lines of the present A53, and the 1 in OS map boldly marks 'Roman Road' along the section below Ramshaw Rocks (023625). However, until the construction of the Leek to Buxton turnpike the route out of Leek was through Meerbrook, over the Roaches and across Goldsitch Moss (p174). It is hard to believe that the surveyor for the new turnpike hit on the same series of straight lines as had his Roman counterpart so many centuries earlier. Wroe and Mellor believe that from Higher Buxton the Roman road set out along the eastern flank of Grin Low (now surmounted by Solomon's Temple) and maintained a generally straight course to join the present Buxton-Leek road near the Royal Cottage (026640). This route would have involved the crossing of numerous upland valleys. In similar terrain in the Woodlands Valley (p40) the Roman surveyors avoided such problems by moving to the other side of the valley; between Buxton and Royal Cottage the valley crossings could have been avoided by moving up the flank of Axe Edge. However, Wroe and Mellor have cut many sections and remain satisfied that the difficult line they propose was the route actually followed by the Romans.

2.6 Buxton to the north-west

The A5002, as it climbs out of Buxton and straightens on the steep south-west slopes of Corbar Hill, follows the line of a Roman road which, beyond Coldspring Farm (044745) appears to have divided. We will first follow the more westerly branch which ran down Goyt's Lane to where Goyt's Bridge (014751) stood until the site was submerged by Errwood Reservoir. As we climb out of the Goyt Valley westwards we are on The Street and the name makes one wonder whether, at least in the minds of those who used this route after the Romans had left, it was looked on as a continuation of The Street from Derby to Buxton.

From Errwood Reservoir, The Street slopes upward to Pym Chair (996767); this chair-shaped stone, now destroyed, was inscribed 'PC'. The final ascent to this old landmark was known as Embridge Causeway. From this crossing of the northern shoulder of Cats Tor, the Roman

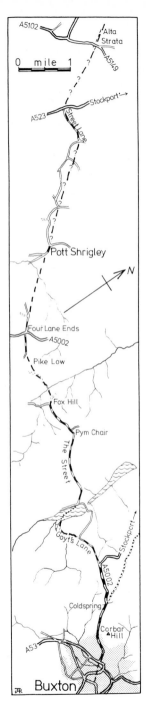

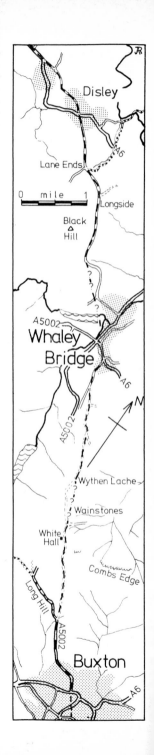

Maps 11 and 12   Roman roads north-west of Buxton.

road probably aimed for Fox Hill (983766) to cross the Todd Brook by Bank Lane (known locally as The Corkscrew) before making in the general direction of Pike Low (967768), Four Lane Ends (962772) and Pott Shrigley (944792). We pick up the definite line again in Street Lane (913818/924817) north of Adlington. As we approach Bramhall there is a fieldname Great Darlingshaw (899838) which can be equated with the 'Derlingesyate' mentioned in 1289 in association with *alta strata*, another clue to the line of the Roman road. Then, nearer to the centre of Bramhall is an old name Street Fields (897854) with Pepper Street (905867/903859) further north leading into Stockport.

The more northerly, and more important, branch of the Roman road that leaves Buxton by way of the A5002 was that to Manchester. About 1½ miles from Buxton, where the present road bears west up Long Hill, the Roman road continued straight ahead; it can be followed, but the narrow tarmac'd lane leaving the main road becomes unmetalled after it arrives at a parish boundary and then, for rather less than half a mile, is very rough; further north it is metalled all the way to Whaley Bridge. After its initial climb, the Roman road levels out on a cut terrace under Combs Edge before losing height to pass White Hall (032764). The road then rises past Wainstones (029770) through a gap cut through the gritstone edge in modern times. The bend to the west between Wainstones and Wythen Lache may not be the Roman line, but this line is resumed below Long Edge Plantation. We are here following the Peak Park boundary and soon come steeply down Elnor Lane and into Whaley Bridge. From there the Roman road climbed to over 1,000 ft on the eastern slopes of Black Hill on its way through Longside to Disley and Manchester.

2.7 Batham Gate

When writing about the Buxton bath in 1572, Dr Jones mentioned that 'Betweene Burghe and it there is an high way forced over the moores, all paved, of such antiquity as none can expresse, called Bathgate'. This Roman 'Road to the Bath' is now known as Batham Gate; indeed, this name appears in a document as far back as 1400.

Following Batham Gate in the opposite direction, we will set out from the site of the Roman station in Higher Buxton. As already stated it could formerly be seen descending near the present railway viaduct at the east end of Spring Gardens. After crossing the infant River Wye, the Roman road climbed steeply again to pass just west of Fairfield church; the route then continued west of, and parallel to, the A6 and some of its kerbs and stone foundations have been traced. This route over Fairfield Common was probably part of the prehistoric trackway (p12) between

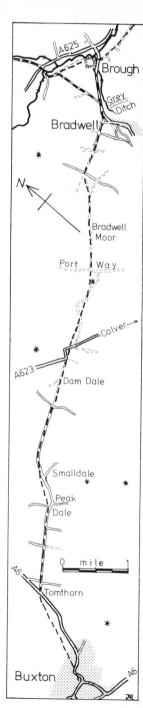

8 The Roman Road known as Batham Gate as it approaches Peak Dale.

9 Roman milestone found at Buxton and now in Buxton Museum; it indicates the distance to Navio (Brough). (*Black's Guide to Buxton, 1875*)

Map 13 Batham Gate from Buxton to Brough.

Arbor Low and the Bull Ring, and a Roman road continues that way to Melandra (p42). Along this road, 1½ miles out of Buxton, near Tomthorn (074760), Batham Gate turns off to the north-east. In medieval times Tomthorn was probably a landmark thorn tree at the road junction.

For over a mile towards Peak Dale, Batham Gate is one with the present road. Dipping into Doveholes Dale we come into a heavily quarried area and the Roman road is lost until we are most of the way up the hill beyond Smalldale. So far we have been outside the Peak Park — the view up and down the devastated valley that we have just crossed reveals the reason; however, beyong Smalldale, keeping up the road to Laughman Tor (102779) we enter the Peak Park once more and, at the same point we can again see Batham Gate before us. A straight mile brings us to a T-junction (111783); Batham Gate kept straight on across Dam Dale and is followed by a footpath, but the only trace of Roman road is a short length of terrace leading up the fields to a double-bend on the A623. The short length of modern road between the two sharp angles of the double-bend roughly coincides with Batham Gate.

From near Mount Pleasant (124788), along the southern flank of Brood Low, past an ancient enclosure (139794), the line of Batham Gate lies mostly in the fields; a section cut here (134792) by Wroe and Mellor showed two successive surfaces, the first of limestone cobbling, the second of limestone chippings. Near its highest point (1,450 ft) the Roman road is visible as a terrace at the top of a field north of the present road, which soon forms a T-junction with the Portway(p17). In another 100 yd, where the Portway keeps straight on north-west, the metalled lane turns sharp right on the precise line of Batham Gate, which can then be followed over Bradwell Moor for a very good mile before the lane veers slightly more east towards Bradwell, whereas Batham Gate follows a more northerly route to Brough. From where the lane veers east, a footpath on the left follows Batham Gate fairly closely; where this footpath rejoins the road at a T-junction (159811), Batham Gate changed direction to come into Brough by Stretfield Road, which is raised above the level of the valley bottom.

Close to where Batham Gate joins the main Bradwell road (B6049), it crosses an earthwork, probably thrown up after the Romans had withdrawn from Britain, known as the Grey Ditch. As we enter Brough, we pass (on the right) an unobtrusive factory. It has a clock ornamented with a Roman soldier, the hour hand is a Roman standard and the minute hand a *fasces*, alternate hours round the clock-face being marked by the letters ANAVIO; these are the letters on the Roman milestone at Buxton, but the 'A' means 'from' — the Roman fort at Brough was Navio.

2.8 Navio and the Long Causeway

The Roman fort at Brough was sited by the River Noe, close to the point where it is joined by Bradwell Brook. A footpath crosses the area where the fort once stood; nothing is now exposed but finds made here during various excavations can be seen in Buxton Museum. Two *ballista* — spherical stones for the Roman catapults — have been built into the fireplace in a nearby house.

Navio stood at the junction of three Roman roads; a fourth road has been traced southwards by Wroe and Mellor up Bradwell Dale towards Windmill (171778). As with Wirksworth folk and the villagers of Middleton, so the inhabitants of Brough used to reckon that their neighbours at Bradwell, a mile distant, were 'different' from themselves, believing them to be descended from prisoners brought over by the Romans from Gaul to work in the local lead mines. We know that prisoners often were *damnati in metalla*, condemned to the metal mines, and that it was customary to locate a military station near the mines; it is quite possible that one duty of the garrison at Navio was surveillance of lead miners at Bradwell. In 1891, when the foundations for Bradwell village school were being dug, a Roman pig of lead was found, and almost up to that year most of the inhabitants of Bradwell — men, women and children — were employed one way or another in lead mining.

The general direction of Batham Gate to the north-east was maintained beyond Navio by a Roman road that, where it crosses the Hallam Moors, is known as Long Causeway. The route out of Navio lay to the south of the River Noe as far as its confluence with the River Derwent. From the B6049 it climbed steeply eastwards and is now a hollow-way up to Townfield Lane, which leads into Shatton (198824).

After it had returned to the valley to cross the two rivers, or perhaps the one river just below the confluence, the Roman road aimed north-east for Stanage Edge. The line is now followed by Saltergate Lane (p 121) from which a footpath branches across Hurst Clough, regaining the lane to Gatehouse Farm (224833). Above the farm there is a good metalled road; the line of the Roman road is followed by a footpath which joins the metalled road opposite a pond. The metalled road then leads due north past the much-modernized Outlane Farm, and as one ascends the hill north of this house the Roman road can be clearly seen just over the wall on the right. It probably continued along the line of the metalled road, and where the latter turns sharply east the Roman road is likely to have maintained its direction along what is now a rough track. It would thus have crossed the boggy ground by the shortest line to reach the firm, well-drained, flank of Stanage Edge — the barrier that the Romans had

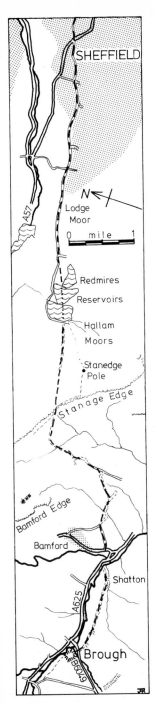

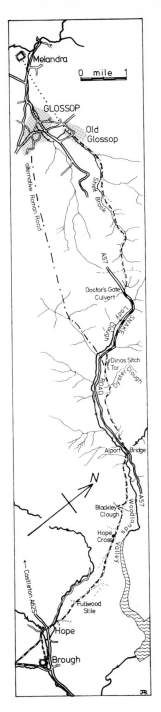

Map 14 (*left*) Long Causeway from Brough to Temple-borough.

Map 15 (*right*) Doctor's Gate from Brough to Glossop.

to surmount to arrive on the Hallam Moors. The whole of this route from Hurst Clough to Buck Stone (231847) is marked 'Ancient Causeway' on the 1840 OS map.

The 1 in OS map shows the Long Causeway crossing Stanage Edge below Stanedge Pole (247845), then proceeding north-east to become submerged in the Redmires Reservoirs. I. D. Margary believes that evidence is now available to show that this is an error; leading up towards Stanage Edge as described in the preceding paragraph, he writes:

> The present track then climbs by a very long slanting terrace but the Roman road did not do this. High up on the cliffs above it another narrower terrace can be clearly seen leading upward at a steeper angle and disappearing through the large rocks at the crest; this is the Roman road.

This would mean that the Long Causeway surmounted Stanage Edge a half mile north-west of the later crossing below Stanedge Pole; it would then follow a line just north of Stanedge Lodge to Lodge Moor Hospital and into Sheffield by Sandygate Road and Lydgate Lane.

Traces of a second Roman route from Navio to Templeborough have recently been reported by T. C. Welsh of Sheffield University. This was a more southerly route that continued from Shatton down the Derwent valley to the Hathersage area before changing course to pass south-east of Carl Wark and across the Burbage Brook (264814); the line then approximated to a length of the abandoned Houndkirk Moor turnpike (281823-287828), continuing to a bridging point (294834) near Copperas House.

2.9 Doctor's Gate

The Roman road that, from Navio, pursued a north-west course to the Roman fort near Glossop, has been known as Doctor's Gate for at least 350 years. This name first appeared in 1627, when there was mention of 'Docto Talbotes Gate'; in the Peak District the word 'gate' often meant 'road', and Dr John Talbot was an illegitimate son of the Earl of Shrewsbury. He was vicar of Glossop from 1494 until 1550 and is likely to have travelled on many occasions from Glossop to his father's castle in Sheffield; presumably he used the length of Roman road from Glossop into the Woodlands Valley that has for so long borne his name.

R. W. P. Cockerton, to whose research over many years we are so heavily indebted, has put forward cogent evidence that Doctor's Gate did not leave Navio by its north gate, as one would have expected, but bypassed the fort on the west. Close to the point at which Batham Gate, descending from Bradwell Moor, joins the B6049, is Doctor's Pasture; the name is no longer used, but the location is known. As we proceed in the direction of Brough, a byroad bears off to the left; at the road junction stood Eden Tree, presumably a landmark and traditionally the site of the house of a Saxon named Eddin. If we take this byroad, we shall find that we are heading straight for Hope church, but there are several things to note before we arrive there. First, there is the site of an ancient bath, reputedly Roman and fed by a mineral spring. Then, just before we cross the brook known as Salt Sitch, we pass over Causeway Meadow, the brook itself being crossed by Causeway Bridge. We next pass Eccles House; this name is derived through Latin from the Greek word for 'church'; the name may be related to the fact that the road leads to Hope church. In 1955 a section of Roman road was uncovered south of the church. On again, and where the road dips to cross the river stood Eccles Cross. The bridge over the river is Watergate Bridge and between there and Hope church, according to the 1847 Tithe Map, was Doctor House. Having established that Doctor House was at one end and Doctor's Pasture at the other end of a causeway that linked the two, R.W.P. Cockerton has a strong case for believing that Doctor's Gate came off the western slopes of Win Hill, through Hope and straight across to Bradwell, without turning aside to Navio. There would, of course, be a road from Hope along the south bank of the river to the Roman station, and a field at the western end of this link-road has the name Burgate, meaning 'the road to the fort'.

It would seem, then, that the road which came to be known as Doctor's Gate bypassed Navio, aiming rather for Bradwell. This would support the existence of a Roman road up Bradwell Dale as mentioned on p36. However the Navio bypass, if one may so call it, also links Doctor's Gate with the Old Portway (p13); from Hope over the Woodlands Valley, Doctor's Gate and this branch of the Old Portway may be one and the same road. Both before the Romans built Navio and after they had finally left, the native peoples would use their own trackway.

This Roman road to the fort near Glossop, the road that has for so long been known as Doctor's Gate, set out from the north-east gate of Navio by the River Noe, which it crossed near Hope. The road then began the long climb up the hillside under Hope Brink; the line is now followed by the lane from Killhill leading under the railway, beyond which it turned to pass Fullwood Stile Farm (172848). From the farm a hollowed lane leads gently upward to the open hillside, where the lower of two tracks continues to Hope Cross (161874), a landmark from which there are very fine views up the Vale of Edale; a little further on, and there is the additional view, in the opposite direction, across the western arm of Ladybower Reservoir.

Half a mile north of Hope Cross the track crosses Blackley Clough; four hollow-ways, worn down by packhorse trains long after the departure of the Romans, can plainly be seen entering and leaving this small clough. The Roman road probably crossed the clough somewhat higher because, from where the descent into the Woodlands Valley begins, there is a much less hollowed terrace higher up the hillside than the track now used, which was improved in 1824 to make a cart-track. Both the Roman and packhorse way lead to a ford above the confluence of the River Alport and the River Ashop; there is now a footbridge.

After it had crossed to the north side of the valley, the Roman road passed through the yard of Hayridge Farm (138896) but the walker should go over the stile by Alport Bridge and follow the footpath across a field behind the farm, west of which the Roman road will be found as a track hollowed by many post-Roman centuries of use. The track leads in and out of a small clough and then maintains a steady course along the hillside before turning to negotiate the deep, grassy-sided, Oyster Clough. While walking easily along this high trackway, one can readily see why the Romans chose to cross to the northern side of the valley at Alport Bridge — their road in this way avoided the numerous cloughs that interrupt the southern side of the Woodlands Valley.

Beyond Oyster Clough the Roman road runs along the lower side of a plantation under Dinas Sitch Tor; *dinas* is a pure Celtic word meaning a hill-stronghold and is a common placename in Wales. Having rounded the Tor, Doctor's Gate joins the A57 about half a mile beyond the Snake Inn, and the main road follows its general line for most of the next two miles, crossing the head of Lady Clough, where there is a sharp change in direction towards the west. In another half mile we arrive at Doctor's Gate Culvert (096929). At this point we turn north along a not very wide path up the gulley — the Culvert — which the Romans seem to have crossed by a bridge; the remains of their embanked road can be seen on the west side where the path goes down to the stream and climbs out again.

The next section of Doctor's Gate, climbing to a height of 1,654 ft, is the best preserved of all its long length. Here is a description of what this Roman road was like over sixty years ago:

> The track is 5 feet below the surface level of the peat moss, through which has been made a cutting 50 feet wide at the top, with sides sloping gently to ditches on either side of the road. The track is constructed of gritstone slabs, the centre stone being 9 inches wide and laid longitudinally. It is flanked at right angles by slabs 2 feet long, 6 inches deep and from 2 to 6 inches thick. The kerbstones are three inches thick, a foot deep and 1 ft 9 in long. They stand about 6 inches above the middle of the road, and the ends of the kerbs, where they fit into each other, are not rectangular but slanting. The width of the road, exclusive of the kerbstones, is 4 ft 9 in; the ditches are 2 feet wide and 18 inches deep.

Today, only a very short section of paving on the summit matches this description; most of the paved way is only a yard wide with all the

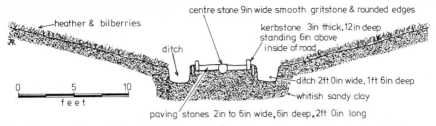

centre stone 9in wide smooth gritstone & rounded edges

heather & bilberries

kerbstone 3in thick, 12in deep
standing 6in above
inside of road

ditch

ditch 2ft 0in wide, 1ft 6in deep

whitish sandy clay

0   5   10
feet

paving stones 2in to 6in wide, 6in deep, 2ft 0in long

10   Cross-section of Doctor's Gate on Coldharbour Moor. (*After W. Smithard*)

paving set on edge, laterally, between the kerbstones. However, Smithard's description of this length of Doctor's Gate sixty years ago equates well with the account of road building given by the Roman poet Publius Statius, who was born in about AD45 and became court poet to the Emperor Domitian. This is how he describes road construction in his day:

> The first task is to prepare trenches and mark out the borders of the road; the ground is then excavated to a good depth. When finished, the trench is filled in with rough material to make a firm base for the road's arched ridge; this is done so that the soil will not give way under the weight of the heavy stones. The road is then made firm with blocks of stone set closely together and firmly wedged. Many gangs of men are needed for this work; some clear away trees and boulders, some bed the stones together, others are busy draining pools and marshes.

11   Doctor's Gate as it climbs over Coldharbour Moor, showing the original paving.

From its highest point, Doctor's Gate descends the valley of the Shelf Brook, but its Roman character is lost. The track has in the past been covered with flat stones, of widely varying sizes, but walkers seem intent on removing these to build cairns; these are quite unnecessary along so obvious a track and the removal of the rough paving is leading to rapid erosion. The track crosses Yellowslack Brook, passes between the steep slopes of Moorside and Shire Hill, and so enters Old Glossop, which lies about a mile north-north-east of the centre of modern Glossop. But we are not yet at the Roman fort (007948), which stood two miles further west on high ground above the River Etherow.

Although the Doctor's Gate route from the Woodlands Valley to Glossop has been accepted as Roman for so long, Wroe and Mellor believe that from the Snake Inn the Romans followed a quite different line. On the basis of field-work they conclude that the Roman road ran above the north bank of the stream up Ashop Clough as far as Upper Gate Clough where there was a change of direction to a fairly straight line over Moss Castle to Wood's Cabin, and through the southern suburbs of modern Glossop.

By what name the Romans called their fort near Glossop is uncertain; when he described the fort in a report to the Society of Antiquaries in 1772, the Rev John Watson referred to it as Melandra, a name that he appears to have invented. There is some evidence that the true name was Ardotalia, but this name has not been generally adopted. The fort was originally constructed with earth ramparts in about AD 80; it was subsequently strengthened by adding a stone curtain wall. The garrison was one cohort of 480 men.

2.10 Melandra to Aquae Arnemetiae

That a Roman road linked the fort at Melandra with the baths at Aquae Arnemetiae was suggested nearly a century ago; more recently (1963) much of its course for the final three miles into Buxton was revealed by aerial photographs, but it remained for P. Wroe and P. Mellor to map the whole of its length and this outline is based on their detailed study.

From Melandra, the road headed south-east towards Simmondley but the precise line cannot now be traced, although several hollow-ways indicate much traffic in this direction during later centuries. From Simmondley a footpath leads to a bend in Monks Road (p 59) and this path may be taken as the general line of the Roman road as far as the point where it crosses the head of Horse Clough; from there the Romans probably kept to higher ground on the flank of Whiteley Nab before rejoining the line of Monks Road at Higher Plainsteads (023912). For much of the way from this point to Abbot's Chair (029903) the Roman

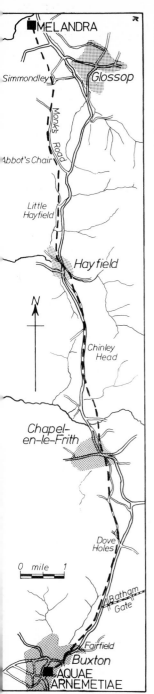

12   Roman road building (*P. Kearney*)

Map 16   Roman road from Glossop to Buxton.

road, now running parallel and to the west of Monks Road, is visible first as an *agger* merging into a wall then as a terrace alongside the same wall's continuation. At Abbot's Chair the Roman line changed direction to aim due south for Brookhouses, Marl House and Little Hayfield; between the last two places, west of the present main road, there is a further line of *agger* and the excavations of Wroe and Mellor revealed a well-constructed road 20ft wide, revetted on its west side as it approaches the stream at Little Hayfield. In Hayfield itself, the Roman road is lost but seems to have followed the street that leads to Kinder before turning southwards to cross the river and climb up a hollow-way in a straight line to join the old Highgate and so reach Chinley Head. For the next mile the present main road is on the Roman line, but the latter then changes direction and passes through Hull End (056827) to Chapel Milton; if, turning backwards from there, the lane that climbs north to Breckhead is followed, the Roman road can be seen as a large *agger* in the first field north of the railway.

From Chapel en le Frith, the Roman road is followed by the pre-turnpike road known as Ashbourne Lane leading over Martinside to Dove Holes. To the west of Ashbourne Lane, just above Lower Eaves farm there is a short but well-preserved length of *agger*. Arrived at Dove Holes, the Roman road changed course at a point close to the railway station; it has been traced as an *agger* leading due south parallel and to the west of the A6. Beyond a low grassy mound, formerly a spoil-heap from lime-working, the line is traceable; it changed direction before joining Batham Gate (p33). South of Brook House, a wall stands on the *agger* and the final visible relic of this Roman road is the lane on the west side of the churchyard wall of St Peter's, Fairfield.

3 The Dark and Middle Ages

A wild way were this, save a guide were at hand
To follow us each foot, so the folk complained.
William Langland,
The Vision of Piers Plowman, c1370

In the Dark Age following the departure of the Romans, the roads fell into decay, as did the Roman towns. An unknown Saxon minstrel has left us his impressions on coming upon some Roman ruins: 'Wondrous are these walls, yet the fortress lies broken, frost enters and towers crumble'.

But neither the Saxons from the south nor the Angles from the east made very rapid headway in the Peak District, where the native British maintained a degree of independence for two centuries after the new invaders began to settle in the south and east. One of the earliest traces of Saxon penetration was discovered beside the Roman road from Derby to Buxton. When a burial mound (149641) near Benty Grange was opened in 1848, traces of chain-mail were found together with a helmet, which is now in the Sheffield Museum. This helmet was crowned by a bronze boar with gold tusks; the nose-piece was surmounted by a silver cross. This reminds one of the story of Beowulf, written in about AD 700: 'The shapes of boars, adorned with gold, glinted above their helmets'. And we know that the West Saxons and Mercians joined forces to fight Edwin, King of Northumbria, somewhere in the Derbyshire hills in the early seventh century. The Saxon burial at Benty Grange is of this period and it is a fair conclusion that the Saxon and Mercian armies marched up the Roman road.

Later, England was invaded by the Danes. In about 877, Northworthy, the Saxon town which had developed near the Little Chester of Roman days, was taken over by the Danes who renamed it Derby. This was just before Alfred the Great drew up the treaty that set the boundary between Saxons and Danes along Watling Street; north and east of this Roman road from London through St Albans and Lichfield to the Severn at Shrewsbury was Danelaw. Some fifty years later we hear of the Peak District for the first time — *Peac Lond*, is mentioned in the Anglo-Saxon Chronicle in 924. Roads are sometimes referred to in Saxon charters: *haehstraet*, which we can recognise as 'high street', meaning a main road;

heiweg, a highway; *portweg*, a way to a market and so, by an extension of meaning, any great thoroughfare. Also of this period is the Old Norse *gata*, meaning 'way or road'; the names of many old trackways in the Peak District include the element 'gate' having this old Norse meaning.

Shortly before the Norman Conquest, the Saxons set out most of the parish boundaries in England, a fact of great importance when tracing ancient roads; just as King Alfred used Watling Street as a definite and clearly visible line for the boundary of the Danelaw, so did the later Saxon bishops and reeves often use old roads when defining parish boundaries.

With the coming of the Normans, and particularly with the founding of the monastries, travelling increased and even if little was done to improve the roads, at least many bridges were built where previously rivers were forded. Accommodation for travellers was, to a great degree, provided by the abbeys, monasteries and priories that were being founded at this time. A charter of 1205 shows that this became organized on a wide basis, for it gave the livings of the Derbyshire churches at Brassington, Bradbourne, Atlow, Ballidon and Tissington to the Prior of Dunstable, on the ground that as the Priory there was 'placed on a public cross-roads of England, they have very many guests; it is seemly, therefore, that they should have some helpers in satisfying so many'.

Yet life in the Middle Ages was still very local; manor and monastery, village and town, were all largely self-contained. Medieval highways were often little more than legal rights of way, but in 1285 the Statute of Winchester placed the responsibility for the maintenance of highways on the landowners in each manor. This Statute also stipulated that when a track or bridleway became impassable, another should be made alongside; thus the medieval ways sprawled across the unenclosed commons and moors. They were nevertheless rights of way for all to use, then as now. One such way passed through the courtyard of Sir Henry Fitzherbert's manor house at Norbury (125423); Sir Henry naturally did not like to see all and sundry passing his windows, but he had to obtain a licence (dated 8 May 1305) from the King before he could divert the old way and then only 'so long as he made another way, through his own lands, equally commodious for travellers'. Then at Atlow (231487), a manor court held on 26 June 1375, directed that 'an enquiry be made at the next court about the blocking up of a path in le Rycroft'. In the Atlow Court Rolls we also read of medieval roads called 'le Thachwaye' and 'Ledeyate'; there are many Lidgate, or Lydgate, names in the Peak District and place-name scholars derive the word from two Old English words — *hlid* and *geat* — which, taken together, mean a 'swing-gate'.

Trade in the Middle Ages was fostered by the establishment of markets. This could be done only by charter, and the earliest such charters for the Peak District were for markets at Hartington in 1203, Chester-field in 1204 and Leek in 1207; others followed at Castleton in 1222, Tideswell in 1251, Bakewell in 1254. Ashbourne market was first recor-ded in 1257. Glossop was granted its charter to hold markets in 1290, Wirksworth in 1306, Alstonfield in 1308 and Monyash in 1340. A medi-eval English lawyer, Henry de Bracton, compiled a treatise *On English Laws and Customs*; this work was completed in 1256 and in it Bracton states that, to be justified, markets should not be nearer to one another than the distance that anyone could travel in a day, adding that a reason-able day's journey is 20 miles. However, the old lawyer realized that more is involved in going to market than getting there:

> The day's journey is divided into three parts; the first part, that of the morning, is to be given to those who are going to market, the second is to be given to buying and selling, and the third part is left for those returning from market to their own homes and for doing all those things that must be done by day and not by night, on account of the snares and attacks of robbers, that all things may be in safety.

Bracton concluded that, to get to market, a person could be expected to travel one-third of 20 miles, say 7 miles. If we now take another look at the markets established in the Peak District in the Middle Ages we shall find that, south of the barrier of Kinderscout, there would be few areas further from a market than seven miles.

In the Middle Ages roads were maintained by the inhabitants of each village through which the roads passed. This duty was enforced by Common Law and there were 'Way-wardens' to supervise this unpaid, unskilled, labour. When it would be to his benefit, the lord of the manor would ensure that a particular road was kept in repair; or perhaps a monastery would have a special interest in a nearby road — as was the case at Dieu la Cresse, near Leek (p54). Edward III gave permission for the levy of a toll to defray the cost of repairing a highway, but this antici-pated the general introduction of this method of fund-raising by four centuries.

3.1 The Saxon Portways

In Chapter 1 we traced a prehistoric north-south route through Derby-shire and mentioned that, in Saxon times, this ancient way became known as the Old Portway. The Old English word 'portway' originally meant a way to a market town and it could therefore be applied to almost any important thoroughfare, ie 'through-way'. There are Portways in many parts of England; the Saxon settlements at Southampton and Northampton were linked, via Oxford, by a Portway that is referred to in the Anglo-Saxon Chronicle as far back as 912 AD. There were cer-tainly two Portways in our own area, possibly three. The Saxons made

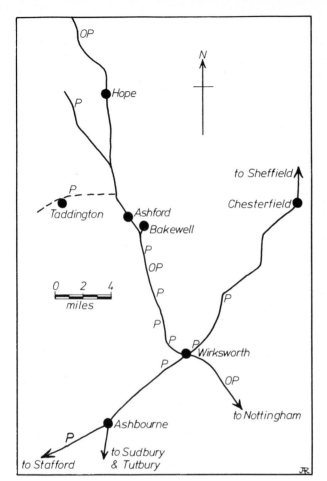

Map 17 Saxon port-
ways in the Peak
District. P=Portway
place name; OP=Old
Portway (Alport) place
name.

good use of the north-south Iron Age route (p13) and would seem to have
distinguished it by the affix *ald*, meaning 'old', suggesting that the Saxons were aware that it was an older way than their Portway that followed the general line of the Roman Hereward Street (p24). The Old
Portway passed over Alport Hill south-east of Wirksworth, forded the
Lathkill at Alport, and eventually came into Alport Dale leading off the
Woodlands Valley. We shall here consider this Old Portway within the
context of the Saxon period; in Chapter 1 we endeavoured to restrict
our treatment to the prehistoric aspect of this route, many lengths of
which are still in use as roads, bridle-ways or footpaths. All who set out
to follow the Old Portway are heavily indebted to R.W.P. Cockerton
for his pioneer researches on this fascinating major route through the
Peak District.

The Old Portway can be traced by place-name evidence from Nottingham, an early Anglian settlement; a thirteenth-century deed relating to land near Sandiacre refers to the 'Portewaye' as one of its boundaries. The next clue is the road still called 'Portway' leading from Coxbench (371435) north-west to Holbrook; 'le Port Way' was recorded for the Holbrook area in 1596. The original Saxon route presumably lay to the west of the present village to ford the Derwent at Milford (351451), referred to in Domesday Book as 'Muleford'. The Portway is mentioned hereabouts in the medieval charters of Darley Abbey. From the ford the probable prehistoric line was over the Chevin and up Longwalls Lane to Alport Hill (305516) and the Saxons are likely to have used the same route.

It is instructive to stand on Alport Hill, a National Trust property, and view the lie of the land. The hill has a steep west flank and the ways ascending from that side have all become hollowed by centuries of use; approaches from the more level east and south-east have been obliterated by cultivation. The precise line of the Old Portway from Alport

13 Longwalls Lane at Blackbrook, near Belper, and its continuation to the south, marks the route of a Portway and, possibly, part of a Roman branch-road from The Street.

Hill into the Saxon town of Wirksworth can only be surmised; there are now two ways and both are old. First there is the present road that sets out due north past Broadgates Farm, along Hay Lane, to Hardhurst and over The Gilkin to arrive in Wirksworth via Washgreen; both The Gilkin and Washgreen are mentioned in the early fifteenth century, and Broadgates was originally Broad Gate — the broad way. The alternative route would have descended from Alport Hill more to the northwest into the old lane just north of New Buildings, proceeding down the hollow-way to Holehouse; the lane (still hollow) then climbs and merges into Pratthall Lane, which leads into Wirksworth via Gorsey Bank and Warmbrook. As the place-names along this alternative route can be traced only to the seventeenth century, the Broad Gate would, on balance, seem more likely to be the Old Portway.

By whichever route the Old Portway entered Wirksworth, it is at least certain that this venerable town was the next place of importance along the Saxon way from Nottingham; the church at Wirksworth contains one of the finest examples of early Saxon sculpture in England, and written records of the town go back to 835 AD. The names of three other Saxon settlements along their Old Portway appear in documents dated 924-926 AD: Badecan Wiellon (Bakewell), Aescforda (Ashford) and Hope (so spelt even in Saxon times). Map 17 shows a concentration of early 'portway' references along a line joining Wirksworth and Bakewell, suggesting that this length of the Old Portway, linking two important Saxon settlements, was of special significance; a thirteenth-century reference to 'the way from Wirkiswrthe to Bathecwelle' lends support to this suggestion. The way out of Wirksworth was through Dalefield ('the Porteway in Dalefield') and would approximate to the line of the present main road up the steep hill to the west, branching in a quarter-mile along the lane to the north-west towards Gallows Knoll; above this lane, in a field on the left (274542) is a rough block of limestone set on end and having every appearance of an ancient marker, unlike the smaller upright block of gritstone in the adjacent field which is clearly a relatively modern rubbing-post for cattle. From the neighbourhood of Gallows Knoll, as we have already described (p 15) the prehistoric trackway on which this Saxon portway was based followed the Chariot Way, passing to the west of Griffe Grange where the 'Porthway' was mentioned in 1260, and descending to Grangemill. The Old Portway, now a farm road, can be seen on the west of the mill-pool; the present road to Winster (B5056) soon rejoins the portway line and passes Ivonbrook Grange, on the site of another monastic farm documented in relation to 'le Portweye'. Then this ancient route gave its name to the seventeenth-century Portaway Lead Mines near the southern end of Islington Lane, named from the lost village of Islington. The lane is now a rough farm road that passes close to Grey Tor, a prominent limestone outcrop. Beyond the crossing of the Elton-Winster road, the old way is known as Dudwood Lane. The section of the Old Portway from the bottom of this lane to its junction (223626) with the Elton-Alport road is now merely a footpath, except for a short length giving access to a farm; it was stopped up in 1816 to force traffic to use the new turnpike (p180).However a good length of paving on the old way is preserved on the steep ascent below Robin Hood's Stride, beyond which the former highway degenerates into a footpath across fields until it emerges on the lane leading to the ancient ford through the Lathkill at Alport; it is of interest that hedge-dating by the number of different varieties of trees supports the view that the lane leading this way into Alport is at least medieval.

North of Alport the Old Portway ascends Dark Lane to Haddon Fields, where it is crossed by another old way(p114)that climbs from Coalpit Bridge; the 1840 OS map marks this crossing-of-the-ways(217-653) 'Two Trees', evidently a landmark, but this name is now applied, wrongly, to the junction (216662) of the Old Portway with the Newhaven-Bakewell turnpike. In a beating-of-the-bounds of the Manor of Bakewell on 13 November 1562, the surveyors came this way, but in the opposite direction, and the boundary was recorded as 'following the crest of Ditch Cliffe to the South End of Burton flatt and so following the Portway to Nether Haddon field gate....' Ditch Cliff and Burton Moor will be found on the 1 in OS map. After crossing Haddon Fields, the Old Portway thus followed the general line of the turnpike towards Bakewell, but, where this road dips to the north-east (at 213673), the portway followed the direct line of the present footpath past Moor Barn to ford the Wye at Ashford, so by-passing Bakewell by about a mile. The Saxons must have made a link-road to their settlement by the river, and as one of the present roads from the Old Portway down to Bakewell still bears an Old English name, Yeld Road (meaning 'the sloping road'), we offer the suggestion that this may well represent the Saxon way down to their Badecan Wiellon.

Reference again to Map 17 will show that no 'portway' records have, to our knowledge, yet been traced along the line northwards from Bakewell to Hope; as Hope was a Saxon settlement, this presumed line of prehistoric trackway must have been used as a Saxon portway, penetrating even further into the surviving Celtic enclaves in the hills around Alport Dale. This same route for a considerable distance north and south of Bakewell again became important in the thirteenth century and acquired a new name, 'Castlegate', as we shall see later (p61).

The branch trackway (p17) from the Old Portway leading to Mam Tor also seems to have been used by the Saxons, but evidence for this rests on the name of one lead-mine only — the Portway Mine (128810).

There is another single-reference Portway at Taddington; the name 'Portaway' will be found on the 1840 OS map and appears to be applied to what is now a green lane just north of the dual carriage-way. This green lane is shown on the 1:25,000 map, leading eastwards from 139713 past Horse Stead, with its old lead mines. Dr J. A. Robey has provided us with a record of a 'Portaway vein' in this same area: '. . . an old vein called Portaway . . . which extends to the West side of John Handley's sough close. . . . Also gave him Horsestead Mine for the use of the Portaway mine partners'. This Barmaster's record is dated 24 October 1824, and so pre-dates the first Ordnance Survey reference. Still earlier, in 1795, the Enclosure Map for Taddington names what appears to be the same green lane 'Ditch Furlong Road'. The existence of a Saxon portway through Taddington is thus still problematical. Taddington was a Saxon settlement and would need communications; there may have been a portway leading to it from the Old Portway — the line of the green lane would have continued through Brushfield (159715) to ford the Wye and climb to Monsal Head. In the opposite, westerly, direction the green lane could have led into Old Coalpit Lane (105703), which the 1840 OS map names 'Lidyate Lane', and Lidyate (or Lidgate) is an Old English place-name (p46). Here, then, is an enigmatic Portway awaiting further research.

It is certain, however, that the Saxons used, and applied their word 'portway' to, the Roman Hereward Street (p24). There are good reasons why this should have been so: Wirksworth, as we have already noted, was an important early Saxon settlement; to the north-east they had a settlement at Cesterfelda (Chesterfield) and to the south-west lay Esseburna (Ashbourne), Staeth (Stafford) and Sudberie. There was a Royal Mint at Stafford in Saxon times, and along the way from there a 'Portway' has been recorded at Uttoxeter, while Calwich Bank, climbing from Ellastone towards Ashbourne, is still called 'Port Lane' by the older inhabitants. The road coming into Ashbourne from the south leaves the Derby-Uttoxeter road (also a Saxon portway) at Portway Head. Proceeding from Ashbourne to the north-east, the next indication of Saxon use is at Breach Farm where there is a Portaway Field (244-534). About 2½ miles north-east of this field, Porter Lane (Porterway in 1415) leads from Middleton Cross (280553) towards the present Wirksworth-Cromford road. If, on the 1:25,000 map, a straight line is drawn from Portaway Field to Porter Lane, it will be found to pass close to King's Chair (252538). If, now, we return to White House and stand near The Stoup (233523), a markstone for a change in direction, provided that a position is chosen to prevent screening by trees, King's Chair can be seen on the skyline to the north-east. There is no evident track across the cultivated fields of Breach Farm, and the hillside below King's Chair is too disturbed by old lead mines for any hollow-way to have survived; it may be objected that King's Chair is a natural limestone outcrop, but it could nevertheless have served as a useful skyline landmark on the way to Middleton Cross and Porter Lane; the skyline outcrop is equally visible travelling from Middleton Cross towards Ashbourne. King's Chair evidently derives its name from its shape, but it is of interest that there was a King's Meadow hereabouts in 1305 and that Hopton was at one time a royal berewick.

Porter Lane, prior to the making of the Wirksworth-Cromford turnpike, would lead into Cromford via Dark Lane. From the ford the Saxons would have followed the Roman road via Starkholmes to Matlock Bank, where there is an old record 'Porteway Close in Mattlock bank'. This is the last portway reference known to us along this ancient way to Chesterfield which began as the Roman Hereward Street, continued in use as a Saxon portway, and for most of its length is now busy with motor traffic.

3.2 The Earl's Way

The Cartulary of Burton Abbey contains a deed, dated about 1200, relating to land near the Abbey's farm at Caldon Grange (086486), and one of the boundaries of this land was *Viam Comitis* — the Earl's Way. Tradition can be very strong in rural areas and this medieval road from Waterhouses (083502) is still known as 'Yelsway Lane'; the older form was 'Yarlsway'. The name derives from the Norman Earls of Chester, who held vast estates in North Staffordshire as well as in Cheshire; the Earl and his tax gatherers travelled along the Earl's Way.

Tracing the route back from Caldon Grange and Waterhouses, it is fairly certain that the Earl's Way climbed to Waterfall Cross (069516), a meeting-of-the-ways and an ancient landmark — possibly prehistoric (p18). The River Hamps was crossed at Pethills ford (now bridged) and the way then went up Longditch, a quarter-mile of hollow-way now overgrown and in some seasons a rivulet; there is a footpath alongside and this brings us to Backlane Farm (056523). The farm road leads into the byroad to Ford, but the Earl's Way maintained its course along what is now another farm road past Bott's Tenement and Upper Berkhamsytch, once an inn, to Bottom House (042527). From the crossing of the River Hamps, the whole line of the old way is a parish boundary which, beyond Bottom House, continued west down the fields, followed by a footpath, to Lower Lady Meadows (027530); the footpath is likely to be a relic of the medieval way. From this point the parish boundary follows the Combes Brook; the Earl's Way probably turned north to Gorsthead Mill, joining the Ashbourne to Leek road at Cook's Hollow (022538) and following it as far as Cook's Lane, which goes off east to Morridge Side. Beyond the lane the course of the pre-turnpike road, which we may assume still followed the Earl's Way, is marked in the fields on the east as a slight hollow flanked by some old thorn trees; this line leads directly into Bradnop (013553) and can be followed into and out of that hamlet as a footpath which reaches the main road again close to Poolhall tollhouse (p142). The main road is carried across a rather deep valley by a nine-teenth-century embankment; the old way dipped north into the valley and can be picked up as a footpath leading past Lowe Hill tollhouse (p143). We are now in Leek, through which the Earl's Way passed; the fifth Earl of Chester, Hugh, died there in 1180.

To the north-west of Leek the way climbed over the long ridge that terminates as the bold escarpment known as The Cloud; a farm by the roadside is Earlsway House (914618). This medieval way may here be following a still older route for it passes close to the Bridestones, a pre-historic burial chamber. From the crossing of the ridge, the Earl's Way descended to the Cheshire plain where, at Marton, there is a reference in a document dated 1313 to 'High Earlsway'.

Along the southern part of the Earl's Way, which as we have seen passed near Caldon Grange, a monastic farm, monks and lay-brothers would travel to and from Burton Abbey. So, too, would the people of Waterfall (082517) when carrying their tithes to Rocester Abbey; the medieval way from Waterfall down to the ford across the Hamps is still called Rocester Lane.

Not far away, above the River Manifold, stood Musden Grange (124-513), a farm belonging to Croxden Abbey. A medieval way led from the grange to Upper Musden (123504) via Abbot's Banks and Abbot's Gate; these names tracing back to monastic times were in use fifty years ago but now seem to have been forgotten. From Upper Musden the monks would make their way over the Weaver Hills to Rocester and on to Croxden; on the way they would join the route used by the tithe-bearers from Waterfall. The way probably descended the old hollow-way of Weaver Lane (not Back Lane) into Wootton and came into Rocester down another hollow-way on the line of Hereward Street (p24).

3.3 A Way from Leek to Macclesfield

When the Earl of Chester transferred his abbey from the Welsh borders, which the monks had found too turbulent, to a secluded valley less than a mile north of Leek, the monks surely rejoiced and the Earl did well to call the abbey 'Dieu la Cresse' — *God prosper it.* The site backed on a wooded hill to break the north wind; there was a bright stream for their water and fishponds, a fertile valley bottom, hills for their sheep, and a little

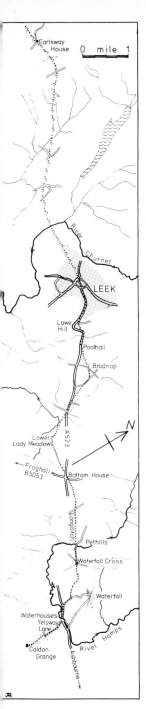

Map 18 (*left*) The Earl's Way.

Map 19 (*right*) A medieval way from Leek to Macclesfield.

town perched on the hill to the south with a church given over to their charge. But they soon found that the valley was apt to flood, and they had to build a causeway across it so that they could get to Leek at all seasons. This became known as the 'Sureway', soon corrupted to 'Surrey'. It is the quarter-mile of road north of the crossing of the River Churnet at Broads Bridge (979572) leading to Abbey Green; the monks had evidently paved this causeway for at the Quarter Sessions in 1724, nearly two centuries after the abbey had been dissolved, the inhabitants of 'the village of Surrey in the Parish of Leek' were judged responsible for the road from the end of 'Surrey Pavement to Gun Gate'.

Gun is the hill that rises to 1,264ft some three miles north of Leek. If we follow the byroad from Abbey Green towards Meerbrook we come to Fould (977587), a farm on the left, and from there a deep hollow-way climbs directly towards the summit of Gun. The hollow-way must be the 'Gun Gate' referred to in 1724, but it was in use during the Middle Ages; we have heard it called the Trusseway, a 'trusse' being part of a packhorse's equipment. Above the 1,000ft contour the ground levels somewhat and the old way is well defined between stone walls; it is very broad but overgrown with tussocks and sallows. It may have been along this old way that the monks of Dieu la Cresse sent wool from their upland granges to Chester for export. In 1280 a merchant living in Florence was importing wool from England and he recorded that his suppliers at Dieu la Cresse produced annually twenty sacks of wool each weighing 26 stones, a total of $3\frac{1}{4}$ tons. To carry this load would have required a train of about thirty packhorses.

Towards the summit of Gun, the old way joins a road coming up from Meerbrook, but where this road bears left to Eleven Lane Ends, the medieval way kept straight on, the line now marked by a wall; this line develops into a rough track down to Gun End (965629). We now have a choice of two roads; to the right past the entrance to Swythamley Hall (974646), which stands on the site of a grange of Dieu la Cresse Abbey; to the left to Bearda Mill (964640). Examination of the ground shows that from Bearda Mill the original way could have continued straight on down the east bank of the stream to a ford, which the present writers have used to cross the River Dane. This would have offered a more direct line to Wincle Grange. Dane Bridge was first mentioned in 1357; before the bridge was built the old way crossed the river here by what was then known as Slider Ford, because the shaly banks were so slippery. As we climb out of the Dane Valley, Wincle Grange (955654) with its ecclesiastical-style windows lies half a mile to the west and out of sight; it belonged to Combermere Abbey in Cheshire. The way past the grange can be followed on foot and beyond Bennettshill (952665) a short length of the old hollow-way leads towards the crossroads below Cleulow

14 Hollow-way leading to Cleulow Cross on the medieval route between Leek and Macclesfield as it would have appeared in the Middle Ages before the cross became obscured by trees. (*R. Hayhurst*)

Cross (953672); this early medieval cross is now almost hidden by a small plantation, but when the knoll on which it stands at a height of 1,170 ft was bare, the cross must have been a very distinctive landmark. The medieval hollow-way can clearly be seen passing to the west of the cross just outside the plantation; it soon joins the road leading through Sutton to Macclesfield. This route between Leek and Macclesfield, although extremely hilly, seems still to have been the usual way from one town to the other even in the eighteenth century; Dr Clegg, a minister and physician from Chapel en le Frith, noted in his Diary under the date 27 August 1731, that he passed over 'Dane Bridge in the road from Macclesfield to Leek'.

3.4 Macclesfield Forest Ridgeway

Macclesfield Forest once included the whole area between the River Dane to the south and the River Goyt to the east, stretching north to Marple and west to Macclesfield. Set aside for hunting, it is mentioned in the thirteenth century; the Master Foresters were the heads of the Davenport and Stanley families.

From Macclesfield, if we set out along the old way to Leek, just described, we can reach the centre of the Forest by turning east by the River Bollin, through Langley (941715). From there Ridgegate, in old times the way to the ridge and now a metalled road, leads to Toot Hill (971-719), a fairly common place-name meaning a lookout point. We are now near the centre of the old hunting forest with Forest Chapel less than half a mile further on. From the little church, where the traditional rush-bearing service is still observed, an old way leads down Oven-House Lane to Bottom-of-the-Oven (979722); somewhere along this lane, perhaps, was a communal bread-oven.

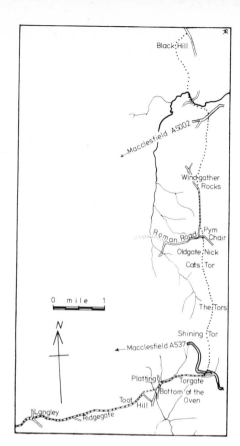

Map 20   The Macclesfield Forest ridgeway.

15 (*right*) Hollow-way near Coombes Edge leading into the Monks Road to Hayfield.

Just north of Bottom-of-the-Oven is Platting, a name denoting a primitive bridge over a stream, and there we join the old coach road from Macclesfield; in half a mile there is an original milestone but of more interest in a medieval context is the nearby farm, Torgate (987725), which means 'the way to the tor'. The 'ridge' of the Ridgegate along which we set out would seem to have been the series of tors — Shining Tor, The Tors, Cats Tor — which define two miles of the Cheshire-Derbyshire boundary and which make an exhilarating high-level walk. Descending from Cats Tor we pass Oldgate Nick; when crossing the ridge, as opposed to walking along it, this would appear as a skyline notch. Less than half a mile north of the Nick we reach the Roman road (p31) at Pym Chair. North again this long ridgeway passes over Windgather Rocks (995783); the line is still the county boundary and continues through Blackhillgate — we have now left the Torgate and are on the way to Black Hill (990824). From Black Hill the ancient way would descend to the Roman road from Buxton to Manchester.

3.5 The High Peak

The ridgeway through Macclesfield Forest has brought us within striking distance of Kinderscout. In the Middle Ages this forbidding plateau was seldom trodden by human feet, but to the west both Hayfield and Glossop were already places of some importance. Midway between them a road climbs round the northern shoulder of Cown Edge before descending steeply into Charlesworth; this is Monks Road, used by the monks of Basingwerk Abbey, Flintshire, which owned land in the area, given to the abbey by Henry II in 1157. It would seem that the monks paved some lengths of their road, for in 1290 one part of it was referred to as 'le Cauce', ie the causeway. By the roadside near its eastern end there is a curiously shaped stone that has been known as the Abbot's Chair (029903) since at least 1640, when it was so named on a map of the area; it has the appearance of the broken base of a medieval cross.

From Hayfield the medieval traveller could also climb over the south-west shoulder of Kinderscout past Edale Cross (077861). Another name for this was Champion Cross, a corruption of 'Champayne', the name of the southern part of the Peak Forest which included much open grazing country; near the point where the cross stands the three forest wards of Longdendale, of Ashop and Edale, and of the Champayne met, and the cross is likely to have served both as boundary stone and guide stone.

16 Medieval stone known as the Abbot's Chair by the side of the Monks Road; the shrine is modern.

17 Edale Cross is much older than the date and inscription, which refer to its restoration. (*P. Kearney*)

Map 21 Hope to Bakewell via Castlegate.

A slightly lower route would have been from Chapel en le Frith up Stonygate past Slack Hall and Breck Edge (082821) then into Edale via Chapel Gate (105838). Continuing east, there was another medieval guidecross, Eccles Cross, at Hope, with Hope Cross (161874) on the ridge between the rivers Noe and Derwent. Several medieval tracks led over these hills to granges owned by Welbeck Abbey; some of these old ways converged at Slippery Stones (168952).

3.6 Hope to Bakewell via Castlegate

We have already suggested that the Old Portway (p17) descended from Bradwell Edge and passed through Hope; we have also described how the south-east end of the road which in the seventeenth century came to be known as Doctor's Gate, made directly from Hope to Bradwell (p39). South of Bradwell the prehistoric Portway eventually developed into a medieval route up Bradwell Dale, following the line of what is now Hungry Lane and Jeffrey Lane into the main road (B6049) as far as Windmill (171778). R. W. P. Cockerton has shown that, at least up to the end of the eighteenth century, this road from Bradwell to Windmill continued as a straight line into Trot Lane (173766), and where this lane now turns sharply into the turnpike road (A623) it formerly kept straight on to the village of Wardlow. Continuing south along B6465 we come to a length of road known as Castlegate Lane. This name 'Castlegate' first appears in documents dating from about 1250, but these relate to a way west of Bakewell. However, it may be assumed that the name was applied at about the same period to this length of road from near Wardlow south to Monsal Head. It is part of the prehistoric Old Portway, and the two or three miles of this ancient way north of Ashford and the two miles south-east of Ashford must have acquired the name 'Castlegate' at a time when some local castle was a place of importance. Just such a castle once stood north of Ashford Church; one of the early custodians of Ashford Castle was no less a person than Edmund, youngest son of Edward I, and in later times it belonged to such historic families as the Hollands and the Nevilles.

What is known of Castlegate? Starting from the direction in which we have been travelling, we first have Castlegate Farm (194755), which lies to the east of the Portway. The late Nellie Kirkham produced early evidence of Castlegate in this area. She quotes a beating of the bounds of the parish of Ashford, undertaken on 12 and 13 July 1570; the boundary followed Coombs Dale to Blagden (near Black Harry, 203745) and continued 'still up onto a little way called Castlegate goeing over the Corner of the hill westward and following the same way towards ffollowe in to a Doble Dyke near to ffollowe towne'; 'ffollowe' is, of course,

Foolow. This 'little way called Castlegate' would seem to have been one of the lanes south-east of the present Castlegate Farm. Proceeding from there towards Monsal Head the way passed Castle Cliff Dale, Castle Cliff Top and Castcliff, and there were fields with such names as Castles, Barren Castle and Castleways Side. The road south of Monsal Head is now called Ashford Lane, but if we choose to enter Ashford from the north-east down a minor road, we shall find that it is marked Castlegate. Passing through Ashford east of where the Castle stood, we cross the River Wye and join the trunk road (A6). This road follows the river into Bakewell, but Castlegate climbed up the little valley due south and is a parish boundary. Not far up this side valley the old way slanted off south-east to what is now a T-junction (204683). The lane descending north from there to the A6 is relatively modern and may be discounted; the T-junction was once a crossroads, one of the ways being Castlegate (here, later called Derby Gate, p74), which continued via Moor Barn (205680). This is now a little-used footpath and beyond the Bakewell to Monyash road this footpath keeps its direct line; this is the length of Castlegate referred to in 1250, when documents describe the location of land by reference to this ancient way. One piece of land was 'on the south part of Edwydale, on either side of Castilgate', the other was 'under the moor, lying on either side of Castilgate, between Edwydale and Outrake'. This 'Edwydale' has been located by R.W.P. Cockerton as the side valley which runs up from the River Wye through Burton Closes towards Burton Moor Farm (223676/210673); in a Rating Survey of 1847 it is referred to as 'Edward Dale'.

We thus have irrefutable evidence that from medieval times that part of the Old Portway stretching for two miles or so each way north and south-east of Ashford was known as Castlegate, and we believe that it was Ashford Castle that gave the way its name. We see no difficulty in the fact that Ashford Castle lay midway along Castlegate, so that a man with his face to the castle would have been travelling north at one point but south at another; there must be many Bridge Streets, for example, that stretch in opposite directions from their eponymous bridge.

3.7 Peakway

An early thirteenth-century charter refers to a grant of lands by William de Ferrers to Thomas the son of Fulcher of Edensor; the boundaries of one parcel of land were 'From King Street by way of Stony Friden Mouth, ascending by the valley to Peakway and along Peakway to the way to Middleton that comes from Hartington'. The charter is in Latin; we have translated *viam de Peco* as 'Peakway', which is supported by the existence of a Peakway Farm near Parwich.

Two of the three ways serving as boundaries to this land can readily be

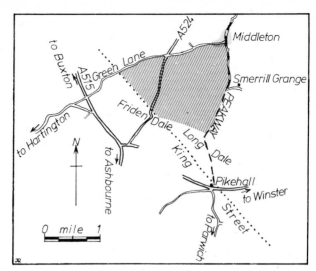

Map 22   Peakway; the shaded area is land defined in a thirteenth-century deed.

identified. 'The way to Middleton that comes from Hartington' is clearly Green Lane (160620-179628) which leads across to Rake Lane and Middleton. Identification of King Street is also not difficult; this must have been the early name for the Roman road now known simply as The Street.

The Street crosses the old way from Hartington to Middleton at 165-623 and, continuing as a straight line south-eastwards, runs into Friden Dale — the 'Stony Friden Mouth' of the charter. A bridle-way follows the bottom of Friden Dale; from the region (185609) where Friden Dale joins Long Dale this bridle-way ascends from the valley (the Latin of the charter is *ascendo per vallem*) to meet another bridle-way leading north to Middleton. There is good evidence, in the form of lengths of hollow-way worn down over the centuries, that this bridle-way leading to Middleton is ancient; this is supported by the proximity of a monastic farm, Smerrill Grange — many granges were thus sited to facilitate communications. From a point just below Smerrill Grange the bridle-way develops into a metalled road, now known as Weaddow Lane, but Weather Way in the sixteenth century. The rich variety of trees in the hedgerow along this lane is a further indication of its long history. From all the evidence, there seems no reason to doubt that the bridle-way from above Long Dale and its continuation as Weaddow Lane follow the line of the medieval Peakway.

There remain two problems. The first is the route taken by Peakway towards the Peak; any solution must await the finding of documentary references to Peakway north of Middleton. The second problem is to link the identified two miles of Peakway with Peakway Farm (173549) which lies west of Parwich; the name of this farm dates back at least as

18   Peakway approaching Weaddow Lane near Smerrill Grange.

far as 1789 and it must be assumed that the name relates to the same way
to the Peak as that passing through Middleton. From the area where
Peakway emerges above Long Dale, a good track slopes diagonally into
the dale and a slight track continues up the other flank on a fairly direct
line to Pikehall; this track out of Long Dale is marked on the 1840 OS
map. From Pikehall the obvious way south would be along Parwich
Lane; the continuation of this lane east of Parwich is now known as
Heavy Lane. Until about 1930 it was a green lane and presumably muddy,
but the OS map names it Highway Lane and it was 'Le Heyweye' in the
time of Henry III. However, although this 'Heyweye' was contempor-
ary with Peakway, it passes 1½ miles east of Peakway Farm. An alternative route to the south from Pikehall would have been up Green Lane,
certainly an ancient way (p70), and over Hawks Low to Peakway Farm,
but we have failed to find any evidence on the ground for such a route.
There is clearly much scope for further research on this interesting
medieval way to the Peak.

3.8 An Old Way from Derby to Manchester

There have been ways from Derby to Manchester since Roman times;
however, the hills and dales of Derbyshire were never easy to negotiate
and over the centuries alternative ways developed, one route, perhaps,
being favoured by the traveller intent on getting north as speedily as
possible, another being better suited to the man needing to call at each

64

village to collect his master's taxes or to sell his own merchandise. The Roman route was still the major thoroughfare in Stuart times (p76), but for much of the intervening period there seems also to have been a way linking more of the upland villages — Elton, Gratton, Middleton-by-Youlgreave, Monyash and Flagg, all mentioned in Domesday Book, and Chelmorton, probably just as old a Saxon settlement but unaccountably omitted. Two medieval landmarks along this route are still known — Middleton Thorn and Chelmorton Thorn. A thorn-tree is long-lived, hardy and not easily toppled by winter gales; in the Middle Ages a single thorn-tree was therefore often planted at a cross-ways or at a change of direction. For these various reasons we propose to treat this Old Way from Derby to Manchester as a medieval route although for the first ten miles out of Derby it coincides with Ogilby's route of 1675, and for another ten miles beyond its parting with Ogilby continues along the old way to Bakewell, which (although much of its length is prehistoric) we have also included in the Tudor and Stuart chapter. And so we will refer the reader forward (pp74 and 76) for the line of the old way north from Derby as far as Grangemill.

The Manchester Road forked from the Old Portway at the point (242-570) where the latter turns down to Grangemill. Walking this way, we once spoke to a farmer repairing the roadside wall and he referred to the old way as the Manchester Road; and we have been told of a Kirk Ireton man, only two generations back, who each year made a journey to Manchester on horseback along the whole line of the way that we are describing.

19   Derby Lane, Monyash, on a medieval route between Derby and Manchester.

20   Guidestone on Derby Lane, Monyash, at the crossing of the Derby-Manchester way with the Cheadle-Bakewell saltway.

21   The old Derby-Manchester way descending to ford the River Wye. The turnpike road of 1810 at Topley Pike, with its present heavy traffic, can be seen top right.

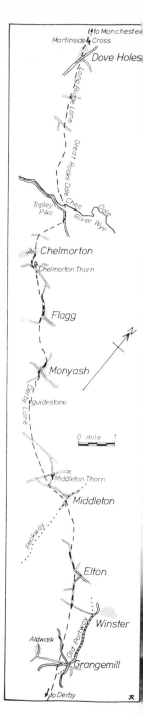

Map 23   A medieval way from Derby to Manchester.

66

From the Old Portway, the first half-mile is now lost; it led in a direct line north-west into Stunstead Lane at the point (236579) where an old way (one length still visible) came down from Aldwark. The northern half of Stunstead Lane serves as a parish boundary and passes Sacheveral Farm; a John Sacheveral was recorded here in 1437. The way continued along Exlowmere Lane towards Elton, then down Gratton Lane to Dale End, where it forded a small stream to pass by Gratton Farm (209618) and slant up the hillside. A footpath further up the lane from the farm will take the walker in the same direction and where the path descends to cross the Rowlow Brook (at 203626), the old hollow-way is very plain. From the brook a lane leads to the site of Middleton Cross (196629), which stood at the crossing of the Derby-Manchester way and Peakway (p62). This old way from Elton to Middleton is shown both on Overton's map of 1712 and Burdett's map of 1762-7 and the earlier map marks its continuation to Monyash. From Middleton Cross the Manchester Road would seem to have continued up the fields to the west, crossing Rake Lane on its way to Middleton Thorn. The 1840 OS map locates this landmark at the next cross-roads (184634), but Thorntree Farm lies a quarter-mile south-west; if the farm is, in fact, on the site of the original Thorn, then this landmark would have been on a more direct line (quite feasible before the Enclosures) from the crossing of Rake Lane to the southern end of Derby Lane, which now begins (167640) as a footpath before coming between walls and leading into Monyash. By the side of Derby Lane there is a limestone gatepost that was an early eighteenth-century guidestone (156651); the four faces read: Buxton; Chedel; Darby; Bakewell. The Cheadle-Bakewell line was a saltway (p123); the Derby-Buxton inscriptions confirm our south-north route.

From Monyash the old way continued past Knotlow to Flagg. John Taylor, travelling in 1820, was told that this was a pack-and-prime way, the green prime-way being for splay-footed oxen drawing carts, whereas the pack-way for horses and mules with their panniers was paved with flagstones about a yard wide. From Flagg the way maintained its general north-westerly line to Town Head, from where it has now degenerated to a footpath leading to Chelmorton Thorn (119697). A road then leads into Chelmorton village and a footpath continues along the west flank of Chelmorton Low into the road to Calton Farm (115719). A short distance down the Buxton turnpike a footpath branches on the right down the steep north-eastern side of Topley Pike (Toppeclyf in 1330) to a doubtless aptly named Slitherford through the River Wye at the junction of Great Rocks Dale and Chee Dale, the site of the medieval Blackwell Mill. This might seem an unpromising way for what must have been a much-used route from Derby and the south-east to Manchester and the north-west, but it is shown by Burdett and by

22   Long Ridge Lane
on the old Derby-
Manchester way.

the Ordnance Surveyors of 1840.

From the ford (alongside the present footbridge) it may be assumed that the direction up the hillside to the north-west is represented by the boundary between Green Fairfield and Wormhill. This boundary led into the southern end of Long Ridge Lane but about a mile of this ancient way has now disappeared in the vast Great Rocks Dale quarries. However, the northern two miles of Long Ridge Lane can be followed from Hardybarn (089752) to Dove Holes. Even there the general direction is maintained, for the old way north from Dove Holes was past Martinside Cross (073788) and Martinside, a hamlet recorded in the thirteenth century. From this point the medieval route into Manchester can be only conjectured; it is likely to have passed Hollinknoll to Lower Crossings, Lidgate and Eccles House, and so through Disley and Stockport.

3.9 Some Other Medieval Ways

It is difficult to point to many other medieval ways in the Peak District, except over short distances; there were, of course, trade routes for packhorses carrying wool, salt and other commodities, but these will be considered in Chapter 5.

Wirksworth was important in Saxon times and in Domesday Book there is a reference to the Danish Wapentake (equivalent to a Saxon Hundred), but this was called 'Hamelestan Wapentac'. In a thirteenth-century deed, land at Carsington, 2½ miles west of Wirksworth, was

Map 24 *(left)* The Alsop-way and other medieval routes near Alsop en le Dale.

Map 25 *(right)* 'The way that lyeth to Tideswell'.

23 Spend Lane probably followed a trackway dating from the Danish settlement at Thorpe during the Dark Ages. In 1738 it became part of the Derby-Manchester turnpike, but was bypassed in the 1760s.

described as lying near 'Homellestonwaye'; in a later document relating to land in this same area, we find 'Hameston Waye'. There is a Hamston Hill (157507) near Thorpe, and one wonders whether the medieval Hameston Way led from Carsington towards this hill. If it did, then Hamston Hill must be equated with the 'Hamelestan Wapentac' of Danish times, and must then have been the meeting place for local government. Some support for this is provided by the Danish name of the nearby village of Thorpe. However, two miles north of Hamston Hill is Moat Low (155540), which may well be a corruption of Moot Low, making it an alternative site for the meeting place for Wirksworth Wapentake. Both sites seem singularly inconvenient, but we can at least say with some confidence that the gated road linking the two sites is ancient. Coming from Ashbourne, Spend Lane brings us close to Hamston Hill, continues north and in another mile becomes Gag Lane, which aims straight for Moat Low. The lane then turns town to the turnpike road (A515), where it now ends, but at one time it continued in a direct line to Alsop en le Dale (161551); the line from the main road is now a footpath. In a thirteenth-century deed by which Henry de Alsop conveyed land to Sir Walter de Lichfield, there is reference to the 'King's Way' and to 'le Ruggeweye'. Which were these ways? More obvious is the 'Alsopewaye' mentioned in a medieval document relating to Newton Grange, just over a mile south of Alsop and now linked with that village by farmtrack and footpath.

If, from Alsop en le Dale, we go up to the Buxton road and follow it northwards for slightly more than a mile, we shall come to Alsop Moor Plantation, a National Trust property. A glance at the map will show that an old road almost certainly at one time ran along the eastern edge of the plantation to its north-east corner, where a parish boundary takes up the line to a crossing of tracks (177583) between Cardlemere Lane (first recorded in 1276) and Cobblersnook Lane, and on down Green Lane to the Roman road at Pikehall.

Better documented are some ways around Tideswell, which in the Middle Ages was a place of importance. First, there is a reference in 1432 to the narrow roadway from Backdale Head crossroads (236736) to Longstone Edge as 'the way that lyeth to Tideswell'. In very early times this way had probably come over the moors to Curbar Gap (261747), down to a crossing of the River Derwent at Stanton Ford (248735), and up the hill through Bramley Farm to the Backdale Head crossroads already mentioned. In later times 'the way that lyeth to Tideswell' could have crossed the Derwent by Calver Bridge, where a predecessor of the present bridge is recorded as far back as the latter half of the fifteenth century, or by the old bridge just north of Baslow Church; this bridge had evidently already been carrying excessive loads before 1500, for in that year an order was made that 'no one shall henceforth lead or carry any millstones over the bridge at Basselowe under pain of 6s 8d to the lord for every pair of millstones so carried'.

The 'way that lyeth to Tideswell' was probably an important medieval thoroughfare, for Tideswell stood astride ways into the Forest of the Peak. One of these ways left Tideswell by Wheston Bank and was known as Kirkgate or Crossgate. If we follow this route the reason for these names will become clear as we pass the base of one medieval cross (140760) a mile out of Tideswell and a complete cross in the hamlet of Wheston; the latter stands a little to the west of the Hall and is a particularly fine example of a medieval cross, Christ crucified to the east and the Virgin and Child to the west. The Middle Ages has been called the 'Age of Faith'; during those four or five centuries the spiritual permeated the secular and no traveller would have passed these wayside crosses without giving some thought to the future of his soul.

24 The fine medieval bridge at Baslow; note the stone ribs beneath the arches.

4 Travelling in Tudor and Stuart Times

It is not the pleasure of the King that this place
should be so bad . . . to my knowledge here have been
swallowed up at least twenty thousand cart-loads . . .
the best materials to make good ground of the place
if so it might be mended.

John Bunyan, *The Pilgrim's Progress*, c1660

When John Bunyan described the Slough of Despond, he was writing from what he knew of the state of the King's Highway around his native town, set in what Daniel Defoe not long afterwards described as the 'clayey, dirty part' of England. Travellers to the north would find the ways less deep in mire once they had reached the limestone and gritstone of the Peak District, but the hills caused them much misgiving. One southerner who rode this way in 1697 noted that 'All Derbyshire is full of steep hills, and nothing but the peakes of hills as thick one by another is seen in most of the County, which are very steepe, which makes travelling tedious and the miles long'.

Travellers and carriers did not get better highways for the reason that the basic principles of road construction had for so long been forgotten. The need had been recognized in 1555 when an act of Parliament made each parish responsible for the repair of highways within its own boundaries. The act laid down that each person holding land of an annual value of £50 and each person 'keeping a draught of horses or plough in the parish do provide one wain or cart... with oxen, horses or other cattle ... and also two able men'; also, each householder had to work four days on his parish highways (in 1563 this was increased to six days). This 'Statute Labour' replaced the medieval 'boon work'; it was supervised by the local Justices and the Act also authorized the annual appointment of two (unpaid) highway surveyors in every parish. Fines were imposed if Statute Labour was evaded; for example, the Court Rolls of the Manor of Tunstall, in North Staffordshire, record that Henry Dowse was fined six shillings for refusing to repair the common ways for six days 'according to the form of the Statute made in the 5th year of Elizabeth', and John Grove was fined three shillings for the same default for three days. Two centuries after the Statute Labour Act, another Act(p131)permitted payment in lieu of actual work on the roads, but by that time Statute Labour had fallen into disrepute — those supposedly doing their six days' stint were dubbed 'the King's loiterers, who work when they list, come and go at their pleasure, and spend most of their time standing still and prating'.

The Act of 1555 must have resulted in some improvement in travelling conditions and in the 1570s Mary Queen of Scots was escorted into Derbyshire in the first coach to have been seen in the county. Queen Elizabeth I travelled with a train of 600 two-wheeled carts each drawn by six horses. Increased travel led to the production of more detailed maps, the first map of Derbyshire being that prepared by Christopher Saxton in 1579, but no highways were marked. The British Mile was defined by Statute in 1593 and ultimately, in 1596, the word 'road' was first used with its modern meaning — until then a traveller merely followed a 'way' or a 'high-way'.

But the art of road making remained rudimentary. Across the Channel, at Rheims, Nicholas Bergier had hit on the idea of learning from the Romans; he studied the construction of Roman roads and in 1622 published his *Grands Chemins de l'Empire Romain* and dedicated it to the King of France. In England, the solution to bad roads was thought to be still more labour and in 1662 an *Act for Enlarging and Repairing of the Common Highways* gave parish surveyors the right to levy a special highways rate of up to sixpence.

Letters had been carried by a system of post-horses since the time of Henry VIII and in 1548 the postage rate was fixed by law at 1d per mile. During the reign of Elizabeth I, the office of Postmaster General became established. In 1663 this office was held by Daniel O'Niel who introduced a postal route from London via Derby and Chesterfield to Sheffield; letters took three days from London to Derby, but only eight hours from Derby to Sheffield. In 1677 a branch service operated between Derby and Ashbourne, but it was not until the 1730s that a cross-country post was introduced from Chesterfield through Bakewell, Tideswell and Chapel en le Frith to Manchester.

According to the historian Stowe, stage-waggons came into use in the 1560s; they had broad wheels to spread the load, but needed six or eight horses to draw them. Regular stage-waggon services for goods and passengers developed between London and cities in southern England and East Anglia. The first stage-coaches came on the roads in the 1640s; they carried four to eight passengers in considerable discomfort and the coaches had no windows! In 1693-4 an Act was passed for 'Licensing and Regulating Hackney-Coaches and Stage-Coaches'. The licence to operate a stage-coach was for one year and cost eight pounds; also, 'no

Horse, Gelding or Mare... be used... under the Size of Fourteen hands high'. In London and for ten miles around the charge for hiring a coach was not to exceed 'Ten shillings for a Day, reckoning Twelve Hours to the Day, and by the Hour, not above Eighteen Pence for the first hour, and Twelve Pence for every hour after'.

But waggons and coaches were now slowly moving beyond the cities. Thus we read of complaints during the Civil War that Royalist soldiers 'did great hurt in plundering the traffique betwixt Lancashire and Cheshire and Derby by robbing and stopping of carriers which went weekly from Manchester to London': their plundering was chiefly along the road between Leek and Ashbourne. Carriers charges were at that time arrived at by bargaining, but in 1692 Parliament laid down that the rates for the carriage of goods in any district were to be fixed by the local Justices.

4.1 Derby to Bakewell

In Tudor and Stuart days the focus of communications in the area was Derby, as it had been since the Romans linked five roads there. This is attested by the fact that in 1577 Derby boasted seven inns; no other town in the county had more than two. There were alehouses in abundance, but these did not provide accommodation. Going north from Derby the next inn was at Mugginton (285432) on the old road to Cross o' th' Hands (283463); in 1601 this was 'Crosse-with-the-Hand', evidently a guide-stone with a pointing hand. The old way to the north from here goes down steeply to the Sherbourne Brook, through Ireton Wood to Kirk Ireton; in a manuscript of 1502 there is reference to 'The gate at the end of the vill of Kyrkyreton through which runs the way from le Peak to Derbye'. The way towards the Peak continued over Moorside and through Callow, and runs down Stainsbro' Lane to Sycamore Farm (267535). Opposite the farm there is now a T-junction, but in Stuart times and earlier, Derby Way (or Derby Gate) here formed a crossroads with Hereward Street (p24); this is confirmed by the guidestone below the sycamore tree, incised on its four faces with the date 1705 and the directions 'Wirksworth, Ashburn, Darby, Bakewell'. The road we are following can be traced in places on the hillside north of Sycamore Farm and soon runs into Tiremare Lane (263541); in a quarter-mile this lane turns sharply north, but the old Derby Way probably continued past Ibet Low (259544) to join the Old Portway (p48). In the eighteenth century, possibly earlier, a length of the Portway west of Bakewell was known as Derby Gate. It climbed due south up a side valley from a point on the A6 almost opposite the most easterly of the Ashford bridges; in the direction of Bakewell the road that is now the A6 had not then been

cut. The name Derby Gate is still applied to the row of houses on the east of the lane opposite the bridge. The lane leads into a wood and peters out, but Derby Gate turned south-east to a guidestone, dating from the early eighteenth century, at what is now a T-junction (204683); this guidestone reads 'Bakewell, Winster, Tidswell, Buxton', but there is now little evidence on the ground either of the Winster road or of the Tideswell road.

One traveller who rode this way was the redoubtable Celia Fiennes, daughter of one of Cromwell's officers. In 1697 she came into the Peak District and visited Chatsworth; she then followed the old road from

25 (*above*) The old bridge over the River Wye at Bakewell.

26 (*left*) Early eighteenth-century guidestone near Bakewell.

27   In 1697 Celia
Fiennes rode up this old
way from Edensor to
Bakewell.

Edensor to Bakewell: 'You descend a vast hill to it, which you would
thinke impossible to go down... if you take a wrong Way there is no
passing — you are forced to have Guides as in all parts of Darbyshire'.
From Bakewell she continued to Buxton and once more noted 'Its very
difficult to find the Wayes here for you see only tops of hills... its impossible for Coach or Waggon to pass some of them'. But in spite of such
difficulties she noticed 'the low drye stone walls' as she rode through
these parts of Derbyshire; most of our walls were built much later,
during the period of the Enclosures (1760-1830), but evidently many of
the fields around the villages had already been walled by the late seventeenth century.

4.2 Derby to Buxton and Manchester

We know the precise route from Derby to Manchester followed in the
Stuart period from one of the maps in the fine roadbook prepared by
John Ogilby at the request of Charles II and published in 1675. Ogilby
surveyed a hundred main roads in England and Wales and drew them as
stripmaps, marking villages, hills, rivers, crossroads, with each mile
numbered. He was the first to use the measured mile of 1,760 yards; to
determine mileages he used a 'perambulator', consisting of a roadwheel
of known circumference and a counting device, which was trundled
behind his coach as he made his survey.

From Derby, the Manchester road is shown as passing by Kedleston
Park to Weston Underwood; Cross o'th'Hands is bypassed on the right,
the road going through 'Ward Yate', now Wardgate (255470). At Lane
Ends (245483) Ogilby shows a crossing with the Ashbourne to Wirks-
worth road, which evidently in his time left Ashbourne via Bradley
Pastures and proceeded to Wirksworth by way of Kirk Ireton. From

Lane Ends the Manchester road continued through Hognaston to Brassington (231543). Except in the neighbourhood of Kedleston Park, the whole of the 1675 route thus far can be followed by car.

The King's Highway passing through Brassington is mentioned in 1663 when the Court Leet directed that 'Everie one everie yeare scowre their ditches adjoyneinge to the King's highway before the first daie of May or else to forfeite 12d'. From Brassington, local inhabitants say that this important coach-road followed the line of the present road past Slipper Low Farm (220569) as far as the T-junction at Rockhurst Farm (216580), where it veered to the left along what is now a wide green lane leading into Hedge Lane and so down to Pikehall Farm (193591). This would seem to be supported by Ogilby's map, which shows a corresponding bend between Brassington and 'Pikeham Inne'. Also, almost opposite Slipper Low Farm there is a Queen Anne guidestone (p83); it is damaged and is now used as a gatepost, but evidently read: Derby; Ashburn; Buxton; Chesterfield 1709. This guidestone has at some time been moved, for it is now incorrectly orientated; its original site was probably at a former cross-roads (222566) a quarter-of-a-mile down the

Map 26   The Derby to Manchester road as shown on Ogilby's strip map of 1675.

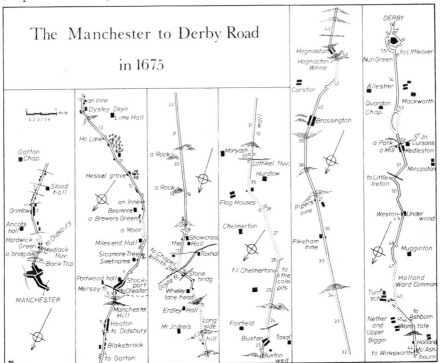

77

28 Guidestone dated 1709 and now
used as a gatepost near Slipper Low
Farm; it is probably a quarter-of-a-mile
from its original site.

road, where a lane still leaves the present road on its western side and
could have led by the ancient Pinder's Lane into an old bridle-way passing to the east of Rainster Rocks towards Bradbourne and so to Ashbourne (as on the guidestone). The opposite arm of the cross-roads
would have led into the green lane that approaches Aldwark from the
west; the way forward to Chesterfield would have been via Grangemill
and along the line of old lanes to Matlock Bridge (p115). At one time
Aldwark had four inns and one of these might well have been the 'Piper's
Inne' shown on the east of Ogilby's road in this area. His 'Pikeham Inne'
is clearly Pikehall Farm which has the appearance of having been largely
rebuilt about 200 years ago, but which still retains a very ancient barrel-
vaulted cellar.

Ogilby shows that from Pikehall the road in his time had a wall on its
west side only. Monyash is marked well off the road to the east, but
Ogilby nevertheless shows the River Lathkill as crossing his road! With
Hurdlow (117667) marked to the west and 'Flag Houses' (136684) to the
east, the road is shown bending sharply to the west as does the present
A515, which the Roman road (Ogilby's road) joined a mile back.

Between Buxton and 'Shawcross', now Shallcross (012797), the 1675
stripmap marks only 'a Rock' three miles out of Buxton, and again 'a
Rock' four miles out. The first of these would be Hanging Rock (028767)
on the skyline west of the Roman road; which was the second landmark
is less clear. A charity of 1674 included a sum of money 'for repairing the

highway from Buxton Butts to the stone that standeth on the hill Cock-ard and so on to Shallcross Brook in June and July' in each year; this charity contributed towards the maintenance of this road until about 1760. At 'Shawcross', Ogilby depicts the hill-top cross from which the place-name derived. The Goyt was crossed by a stone bridge and then the Roman road was still followed over Longside, descending past 'an Inne' to 'Dysley Deyn'. The way continued via 'Hesselgrove', through 'Stockport alias Stopford', past 'Ancots Hall' into Manchester.

The most interesting feature of Ogilby's stripmap is that in 1675 so much of the Derby to Manchester road through the Peak District was the road used by the Romans, which was itself for part of its length based on a way followed before history began.

29   Pikehall Farm, standing at the focal point of several ancient ways, was 'Pikeham Inne' in 1675.

4.3 Derby to Beresford Dale

Izaak Walton wrote *The Compleat Angler* in 1653; it was an immediate success and by 1676 had run into five editions. For the fifth edition, Charles Cotton of Beresford Hall, near Hartington, wrote an adden-dum on 'How to angle for trout or grayling in a clear stream'; this was introduced by a dialogue between *Piscator Junior* (The Angler, Charles Cotton), and *Viator* (A Traveller), which tells how these two rode from Derby through Ashbourne to Beresford Dale.

The Traveller was from Essex and was bent on business in Lancashire.

Cotton overtook him near Brailsford; evidently the route from Derby to Ashbourne in the seventeenth century was much as it is now, except that it was then 'a large measure of foul way'. Cotton pointed out that this proved how much the road was used, 'which is also very observable by the fulness of its road, and the loaden horses you meet everywhere upon the way'. And so they came down Spittle Hill, named from a medieval hospice, into Ashbourne, where they drank a tankard of ale at the Talbot.

From Ashbourne the route was along Spend Lane and then over the hills to Milldale (139547), which they reached by descending the steep zigzags to the packhorse bridge over the River Dove. Their conversation, condensed somewhat, went like this:

Viator:	I think it the strangest place that ever men and horses went down; the safest way is to alight.
Piscator:	I think so too, for you who are mounted on a beast not acquainted with these slippery stones; and though I frequently ride down, I will alight too, to bear you company.
Viator:	It is as steep as a penthouse.
Piscator:	To look down from hence it appears so; but the path winds and turns, and will not be found so troublesome.
Viator:	These stones are so slippery I cannot stand. What's here, a bridge? Do you travel in wheelbarrows in this country? This bridge was made for nothing else — 'tis not two fingers broad.
Piscator:	I have rid over the bridge many a dark night. You are safe over, and now you are in Staffordshire.
Viator:	Pray what do you call this hill we came down?
Piscator:	We call it Hanson Toot.

And so, safely down the zigzags, which in those days were evidently so much used that the way was worn to the bare rock, and over the packhorse bridge that has ever since been known as Viator's Bridge, the two travellers rode up Mill Lane to Alstonfield. From there they would follow the old road down Narrowdale (125574) and so come to Beresford Hall, Charles Cotton's home, which most regrettably was demolished in about 1900.

5 Packhorse Ways and Drovers' Roads

. . . they used to see the pack-horses and hear the tinkling of their bells on this very highway.

George Eliot, *Felix Holt*, 1866

PACKHORSE WAYS

From the early Middle Ages until the seventeenth century, the packhorse and packmule were, more often than not, the sole means of transporting merchandise; even in the mid-nineteenth century strings of packhorses were still common in the Peak District, for they could travel over the moors much more readily than could heavy waggons, even though these had six horses to pull them. One breed of packhorses much favoured was the Galloway, small but strong and used to rough country; there was also the Jagger-galloway. *Jaeger* is the German word for a hunter, but the German Jaeger-pony was a very different animal from the hunter as we know it in England. That the German Jaeger-pony became very common in the Peak District and further north is made evident by the fact that in these areas the man in charge of a train of packhorses became known as a 'jagger'; the name is ancient for a document of 1306 relating to Little Longstone refers to Thomas le Jager.

The packhorse's load was carried in two panniers or baskets, one slung on each side of a type of saddle called a 'crook'. Coal from the Lancashire pits, for example, was carried in baskets 30 in deep, 20 in long and 10 in wide; in a pair of these baskets a packhorse could carry 2½ cwt of coal. But in the earliest days of the packhorse the commodity most commonly carried over long distances was salt; the routes followed became known as saltways (p119).

One of the early carriers by packhorse was Thomas Pickford who lived at Poynton, Cheshire, in the seventeenth century; during the Civil War he was charged with supplying horses to the Royalists and Cromwell deprived him of his small estate. After the Restoration he resumed his business as a carrier and in addition acquired a stone quarry in the Goyt Valley, carrying the stone by packhorse for the repair of roads around Manchester. One would like to be able to relate this Thomas Pickford to the James Pickford, also of Cheshire, from whom the world-

famous transport company traces its descent; unfortunately, there would seem to be no documentary evidence that the seventeenth century Thomas was a forebear of the eighteenth-century James.

Packhorses generally travelled in 'trains' and it was not uncommon to see forty to fifty in single file. A packhorse's harness often included one or more bells; travellers and the leaders of other trains were thus warned of their approach. This was necessary for packhorse ways were usually too narrow for two horses to pass.

It is surprising how quickly well organized packhorse trains could travel over long distances. The best example is provided by some of the 'fish-trains'. Daniel Defoe, writing in about 1700, tells us: 'The Workington men carry salmon, fresh as they take them, up to London, where the extraordinary price they yield — from 2/6 to 4/- per pound — pays very well for the carriage. They do the same from Carlisle'. Defoe does not state how long the journey took, but if, arrived in London, the salmon were still 'fresh as they take them', it could not have exceeded four days. But these fish-trains plodded along night and day with many changes of horses and needed to maintain an overall speed of only 3mph. Their route south would take them down the western side of the Peak District, probably through Whaley Bridge and Buxton.

In the Manchester area, until about 1750, the textile industry depended on the packhorse. The manufacturers sent out their travellers on horseback to take orders, and chapmen with trains of packhorses then distributed the finished products and brought back wool or other commodities. Samuel Smiles tells us that one Manchester merchant sent cloth goods over the Derbyshire hills to Nottingham, Lincoln and Cambridge; the packhorses returned with wool, malt or even with feathers! The merchant himself was on horseback for the greater part of each year taking orders and receiving payment in golden guineas 'travelling along bridle-ways, thro fields where frequent gibbets warned him of his perils'.

The ways used by the packhorses were roughly paved, at least over parts of their length. Sometimes they ran alongside a haulage way along which oxen could draw carts; this would be left unmetalled, the cloven hooves of the oxen splaying out to sustain them over soft ground where a horse would quickly become bogged. The lengths over soft ground that were paved for the packhorses were often known as 'causeways' or 'causeys', from the Old French *caucie*, which in turn derives from a Latin word meaning 'trodden'. The causeway would only be about two feet wide and would therefore be much cheaper to make and maintain than a full-width road; parishes would often accept responsibility only for the repair of a 'pack and prime way', as such ways were sometimes called. Another merit of the packhorse was that rivers could be crossed by quite narrow bridges, and these could be steeply humped to leave plenty of freeway for the river in times of flood; the earliest of these packhorse bridges are medieval.

Where a packhorse bridge still exists, even if widened to take wheeled traffic, it provides indisputable evidence of a packhorse way; indeed, two or even more such ways may converge at the bridge. They also often converge at a gap in a gritstone edge, as at Curbar Gap (261-747). There is often equally definite evidence of former packhorse ways on steep hills, where the horses had to zigzag to ease the gradient and where rain has washed down for centuries to create hollow-ways. Defoe described one such very steep hollow-way in the Pennines as being 'so narrow and so deep a hollow place... whence the water descending from the Hills made a Channel at the bottom and looked as the beginning of a River'. When the original way became virtually impassable, the leader of the packhorses would start an alternative way alongside; up many peaty hillsides, two, three or even more hollow-ways can be seen. The word 'hollow' is sometimes found as an element in a place-name: Holloway, Hollowford, Hollow Gate, all indicate old packhorse ways. In the Peak District the word 'jagger' (p81) is also found: Jaggers' Lane, Jaggers' Clough, Jagger Way. Then there is the occasional Packhorse Inn to show us that we are on some old packhorse route.

In the Peak District, anyone seeking these old trade routes is greatly assisted by the guidestones erected in the early eighteenth century by the direction of Parliament. The Order Book for Quarter Sessions, Derbyshire, for the year 1709, includes the following entry: 'Whereas in and by an Act of Parliament made in...[1702]...for enlarging Common highwayes... it is therein Enacted for the better convenience of travelling in such parts of this Kingdome which are remote from townes... that there shall be in every Parish or plaice where two or more Cross highwayes Meet, Erected or fixed by the Surveyors of the highwayes... a Stone or Post, with an Inscription thereon in large Letters, containinge the name of the next Markett Towne to which each of the said Joyning highwayes Leads... And whereas the said Act of Parliament hath not beene effectually put in Execution... it is ordered by this Court... that this order and precept be Printed and be distributed to all and every the Supervisors of ye highwayes.'

As we shall find later in this chapter, many of these guidestones remain in position; some have been removed and used as gateposts. Many are dated and confirm that few of the parish surveyors of highways took note of the Act when it was passed in 1702 as this date is rare; indeed in remote villages the surveyors may well never have heard of the Act. But when, in 1709, Quarter Sessions circulated copies of their order that the Act be implemented forthwith, guidestones were speedily erected. Since at that period wheeled traffic over our hills and moors was unknown, it can be accepted that these Queen Anne guidestones were erected on the major packhorse routes. A few of the guidestones have a pointing finger alongside the name of each town, but most merely have the town's name; where the guidestone is in its original position, our observations suggest that the name of each town faces the direction in which that town lies.

5.1 From the Ecton Copper Mines

The copper mines at Ecton (096584) in the Manifold Valley, were worked from the seventeenth century until 1888. In the very early days the ore was carried by packhorse to be smelted at Ellastone, then later at Denby, about three miles east of Belper; the route to Denby was via Newhaven. However, from 1770 onwards the ore was smelted at Whiston (041473), above the Churnet Valley; the Duke of Devonshire, who owned the Ecton mines, had chosen Whiston for his smelting works as being near to his coalpits at Foxt Wood and Hazlescross, both on the Cheadle coalfield. Trains of up to seventy packhorses (Farey states that they were mules) were at first used to carry the ore and the route that they followed is known from a map of 1769 and from local tradition. The map shows two routes: the first from Ecton via Warslow, Onecote, Ipstones and Froghall to Whiston; the second from Ecton via Wetton Mill, Hillsdale, Winkhill Bridge, Bellyband Grange and Windyway Cross to Whiston. As the Whiston works was not built until the year following the date of this map, the two routes were evidently in the nature of preliminary plans and it is fairly certain that it was the second route that was actually followed; it would soon be realized that the alternative route was three miles longer and involved a quite unnecessary descent into the Churnet Valley at Froghall with a correspondingly steep climb out again to Whiston. It is possible, of course, that after the packhorses had unloaded their ore at Whiston, they would go down to Froghall so that their panniers could be filled with coal from the Duke's pits for their return journey; no packhorse travelled with empty panniers if this could be avoided. The average cost of carrying ore in the early nineteenth century was 1s per ton per mile.

Following the route from Ecton in more detail, the way as far as Wetton Mill (095561) is sufficiently obvious. An estate map of 1617 shows no bridge at Wetton Mill although Darfur Bridge, half a mile downstream is marked. By 1770, however, when the packhorse trains began to come this way, there would have been a bridge at Wetton Mill; it is recorded that a bridge there was swept away by floods and was rebuilt in 1807, by the Duke of Devonshire at a cost of £184; the road from Ecton to Wetton Mill had been maintained at the Duke's expense since 1770. Having crossed the Manifold, the packhorses turned along the north side of the Hoo Brook; the route is now a footpath. About a mile up this side valley, the old bridleway that links Grindon and Warslow in a straight line is crossed, and at the same point the Hoo Brook is left, another little valley leading forward and upward to Hillsdale Hall (079-554), which bears the date 1620. The packhorse route came between walls to enter the farmyard of the Hall from the north. Continuing from Hillsdale Hall a hollow-way can be seen in a field north of the lane leading to Grindonmoor Gate, near which is The Pen, once a stockyard for ore and coal. From Grindonmoor Gate the packhorse way has become a metalled road and this can be followed past Felthouse to Waterfall Cross (069516), which, as we have already seen, was once an important landmark; the farmhouse there was formerly an inn. The packhorses then went due south down Benty Grange Lane. On the east of this lane, just before it joins the A523, is a narrow strip of land — a 'slang' — walled off from the remainder of the field; this was a grazing area for the packhorses.

From the other side of the main road, the packhorse way led to a ford

31 Windyway Cross on Ipstones Edge, a markstone for packhorse trains carrying copper ore to Whiston.

Map 27   Packhorse routes from Ecton and Mixon to the Whiston Copper Works; the Casey is also shown.

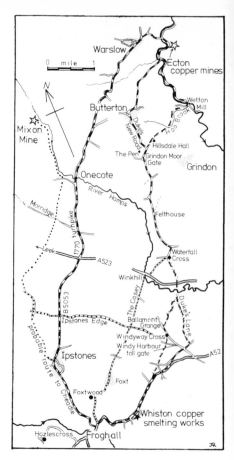

32   Built-up gateway leading to a hollow-way from Onecote over Morridge on the route from Mixon copper mine to Whiston.

(now a bridge) across the River Hamps, beyond which the line is followed, roughly, by a footpath leading over the railway in the direction of Ballamont Grange (059496); this is the 'Bellyband Grange' of the Ecton to Whiston Map of 1769 — evidently the map was drawn by someone more familiar with the harness of packhorses than with Norman French! About 300 yd up the road from Ballamont Grange the packhorse way is marked by a field wall and can be followed by a footpath to Windyway Cross (058490); this 'cross' is a tall stone placed on the skyline as a marker when these hills were unenclosed. From the markstone, the packhorse way is established by a straight field wall with a footpath on its north side. The line aims directly at the site of the Whiston copper works, and for the final mile coincides with the A52.

The Duke of Devonshire ceased to maintain the road from Ecton to Wetton Mill in 1826. The old packhorse route from Wetton Mill to Grindon Moor was too steep for a cart-way and the later route left the

Manifold at Swainsley, where a Stamps Yard had by this time been established for crushing the ore, and followed the lane to Butterton. From there the Duke of Devonshire had to improve the rough track marked on Yates's Map of Staffordshire (1775) leading towards Grindonmoor Gate and the road became known as the Duke's New Road; it is now called Pothooks Lane. Another modification was necessary beyond the River Hamps; an easier way was made and soon acquired the name of Duke's Lane, from the fact that the Duke of Devonshire's copper ore was carried that way. Duke's Lane climbs south from the modern bridge (068506) over the Hamps, crosses the railway and joins the old Cauldon to Whiston road at Park View Farm (066487); local people say that one object of this route was to avoid paying tolls at Windy Harbour tollgate (062488).

5.2 Mixon to Whiston

Copper mines at Mixon (046573) were worked intermittently from about 1730 until 1858. At first the ore was probably carried by packhorse to the Cheadle Copper Works, but after the 1820s the ore was taken to the copper works at Whiston. For information on the route followed by the packhorse trains we are indebted to Mr S. Fern of Onecote.

From Mixon to Onecote the way followed the line of the present farm road above the River Hamps, but then turned southwest; about midway between Onecote New Hall and the turn down to Onecote Grange, a pair of stone gateposts in the wall on the west side of the road indicate the start of the climb over Morridge. The way between the gateposts is now built up but clearly led into a broad hollow-way lined with beech trees; it is shown on Yates's map of 1775. The way ahead led between Hopping Head Farm and the ruins of Willow Meadow Farm; there is no footpath but, with permission, some lengths of packhorse hollow-way may be traced if care is taken to discount several deep natural watercourses that have also cut into the hillside.

Arrived on Morridge the way descended to the Leek-Ashbourne road and from there probably continued through Lower Lady Meadows (026-530) before climbing to Ipstones Edge, which could be followed to join the copper-route from Ecton (p84) at Windyway Cross.

5.3 The Casey

If, from Waterfall Cross, we follow Bromleyhedge Lane down to Winkhill and turn right at the main road we soon reach the River Hamps at Winkhill Bridge and can then immediately turn left on a road which climbs straight over Ipstones Edge. Beyond the point at which the railway and Ellastone turnpike are crossed, the road over the high ridge is the Casey; this is a corruption of 'causey' or 'causeway', indicating that at one time it was a narrow paved way for packhorses, perhaps carrying coal from the pits around Foxt (035486). To the south-west of Foxt, traces have been seen of a paved ford through the Churnet where the river flows through Bolton's Copper Works; mention is made of a ford at Froghall in a document of 1455.

5.4 Alstonfield

The parish of Alstonfield (131556) once covered a vast area and, as we have seen, a market was held there in the Middle Ages. One would expect to find several packhorse ways converging on this very pleasant village. The most obvious is Millway Lane, coming up past the church from Milldale. However, this lane did not always curve round the east and north sides of the churchyard, as now, but ran along the south side to join Back Lane; there was a crossroads south-west of the church. It was up Millway Lane that Charles Cotton and Viator rode from Ashbourne to Beresford Hall in the seventeenth century (p80).

Working clockwise from Millway Lane, the next way leading into Alstonfield is the hilly road from Ilam through Damgate. At Stanshope (127542) the old packhorse way bears right as a green lane leading to Dale Bottom, and from there zigzags up the steep hillside opposite; it is now a footpath and leads across fields into Alstonfield via the former crossroads south-west of the church.

A way from the west is through Grindon and into the Manifold Valley at Weag's Bridge (100541), on the east of which the road makes a zigzag climb, very likely on the same line as that followed by the packhorses. The way ahead to Hopedale (123550) is by the deeply-hollowed Wall Ditch (118548). Towards the top of the hill above Hope (125552) the old way was along Back Lane; the short length of road from Top of Hope direct into Alstonfield was not cut until after the enclosures, as is indicated by the correspondence of the lines of wall on the two sides of the road.

To the north, the old way from Alstonfield was down Narrowdale (125574) and this was the route of Charles Cotton and Viator.

If we leave the village by the road leading to Lode Mill but take the second rough lane (usually muddy) on the left, we are on Gypsy Lane which leads to Gypsy Banks, once a rendezvous for the romanies with a magnificent and unusual view of the River Dove as it flows below Iron Tors. The packhorse way down Gypsy Banks to Coldeaton Bridge is a series of zigzags. The packhorses would have had to ford the shallow river before continuing up the dry gorge to Lees Barn (157567); from there the route would seem to have joined the ancient way alongside Alsop Moor Plantation (p70). An Alstonfield deed of 1687 refers to land

33 Millway Lane
from Milldale to
Alstonfield.

Map 28 The old road
system at Alstonfield.

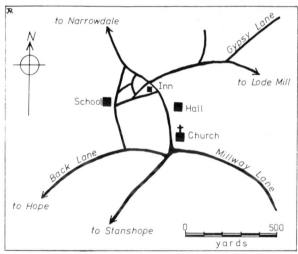

'by the lane leading to Bakewell' given by a local man named Bowman
for use as a Quaker burial-ground; the first stone barn on the left along
Gypsy Lane is still known as Bowman's Barn, so we can say that this lane
is at least 300 years old and led to Bakewell.

5.5 Hartington

This attractive village has a history similar to that of Alstonfield; during
the Middle Ages each had its market and was the centre of a very extensive parish. Packhorse routes must have converged on Hartington as on
Alstonfield, and as late as 1708 the way into Hartington from Hulme End
crossed the Dove by 'a stone bridge for horses'. To the east, the old way
was up the hill past the Hall and through Heathcote. Beyond the Buxton
road (A515) the way led into Green Lane, which continues until it forms

a crossroads with the A524, beyond which Rake Lane leads down to Middleton by Youlgreave (195632). This 'way to Middleton that comes from Hartington' was already well-known seven centuries ago (p62).

   Another likely packhorse route from Hartington would lead to Wirksworth. This way also started past Hartington Hall, but 200 yd past the hall a lane leads to Biggin (155594). From the crossing of the Buxton road the way ahead would be along the remarkable series of lanes — Cardlemere Lane, Cobblersnook Lane, Minninglow Lane, Gallowlow Lane — which link to form a straight line aimed in the general direction of Wirksworth. Prior to 1770, copper ore from Ecton was probably carried this way to be smelted at Denby (397463).

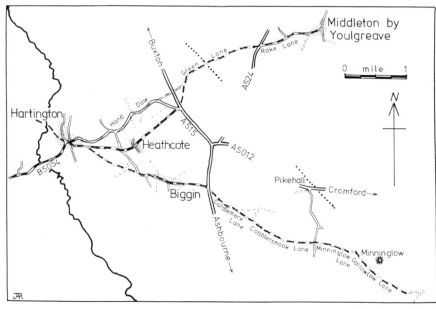

Map 29   Packhorse ways from Hartington.

34   Cardlemere Lane on the packhorse route from Hartington to Wirksworth.

Several people living near this old packhorse way have told us of a train of packmules becoming snowbound somewhere between Pikehall and Biggin, their carcasses and panniers not being recovered until the following spring. 'Starving to death', the local phrase for 'freezing to death', was not uncommon on these exposed hills. In 1692 John Webster, of Hognaston, and his six packhorses travelling from Derby, starved to death in the snow between Pikehall and Hurdlow; this did not deter other members of his family from continuing to ply their trade — a Joseph Webster of Hognaston is listed as a carrier to Derby as late as 1895. Another starving to death is recorded in the Monyash parish register for 1772, when John Allcock and Richard Boham died on Middleton Moor in a snowstorm as they were returning from Winster market.

5.6 Longnor and Monyash

Upstream from Hartington there are four certain crossings of the Dove by packhorse ways. The first is the ford at Pilsbury (116633), but this will be discussed under Saltways(p123).The second is at Crowdicote, where there is a Packhorse Inn; however, in packhorse days the inn was the adjacent cottage. The original 'Crawdy Coat Bridge' was no more than a wooden footbridge; it was rebuilt as a stone packhorse bridge in 1709 and one of the ways that came over it would be from the Royal Cottage (026640) on the Leek to Buxton road, through Longnor, where fairs were held 'for sheep, cattle and pedlary'. From Crowdicote the way east would be through Monyash and up Horse Lane to Ashford or Bakewell. As in the preceeding section mention was made of deaths in snowstorms, and it is of interest that on the highest part of this old way, the crossing of Bareleg Hill (028641), six snow-stones, set up to mark the edge of the road, still stand by the roadside.

A well-preserved narrow hollow-way between walls leaves this Longnor-Leek road at 054643 and climbs over Barrow Moor to Marnshaw Head (Mount Shaw in 1840); from there the old way is discernible down the valley-side to the River Manifold, where there is a footbridge, and so by Ballbank up to Fawside Edge. There are other obvious crossings of the Manifold through a higher ford (052653) and over the same Edge to Hollinsclough.

Also from Barrow Moor an old way, now tarmac'd, leads to Shining Ford (065638), a crossing of the Oakenclough Brook; many fords have acquired this name from the glitter of the water as the traveller approaches — a Shining Ford between Ashbourne and Wirksworth is documented back to 1305. From the Oakenclough Brook ford the way climbed to the road linking Newtown and Fawfieldhead, and from the latter hamlet a deeply hollowed road leads down to, and across, the

Warslow road. This cross-roads is marked on the 1840 OS map as Cross Gates; one 'gate' would be the way just described, leading to Ludburn Ford, the other would be the old way from Longnor to Warslow that

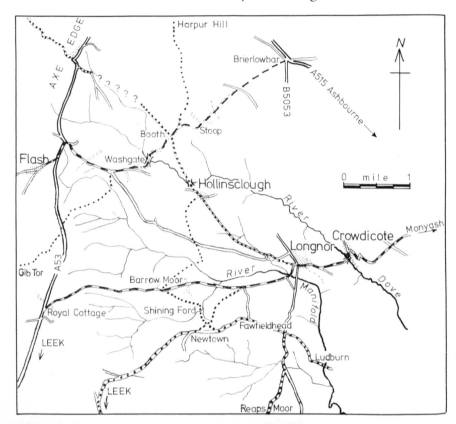

Map 30   Packhorse ways in the upper Dove and Manifold valleys.

35   The Longnor-Leek packhorse way at Lane Farm, near Newtown.

crosses Reaps Moor then turns past Cuckoo Stone (078607) and over the eastern flank of Revidge.

In packhorse days the most important route from Longnor to the south-west would be the direct way to Leek. This set out from Longnor on the same line as the way leading to the Royal Cottage, but after a mile, at the point where there is a T-junction leading to Fawfieldhead, packhorses making for Leek would bear left along what is now marked 'No Through Road'; for the first half-mile the way is tarmac'd, but then changes to a deep unmetalled hollow-way as far as Lane Farm (dated 1759), from where the way ahead leads to Newtown (060631). The route followed the line of the present road over the north flank of Lady Edge to Blake Mere and the Mermaid Inn (037604), and via Thorncliff to Leek. This can be a lonely way even today and few would wish to become benighted there. In 1679 a woman pedlar travelling this way from Leek market to Bakewell market was robbed and strangled by an ostler from Leek named Andrew Simpson, who threw her body into Blake Mere; a century later, John Warltire, an itinerant lecturer in the natural sciences, narrowly escaped being murdered during a night spent in a wayside inn as he journeyed from Bakewell to Leek.

The third crossing of the Dove in its upper reaches was by the packhorse bridge (063668) rather more than a quarter-mile north-west of Hollinsclough. There is some good paving on the steep ascent from the bridge on the Derbyshire side; the track then rakes steadily upwards to Fough Farm and Booth, where it crosses the way from Washgate and leads over Axe Edge into the Goyt Valley.

36 Washgate Bridge crossing the River Dove north of Hollinsclough.

37 Paved packhorse way leading from Washgate into Derbyshire.

The bridge nearest to the source of the Dove was at Washgate (052-674) where there is a perfect packhorse bridge having a span of 21 feet and with its original parapets, 4ft 6in apart and sufficiently low not to obstruct the panniers of the packhorses. Two ways lead down to Washgate from the Staffordshire side of the stream, one from Moor Side on the south, the other from Golling Gate on the west and the ridge road from Flash Bar to Longnor. Arrived on the ridge, the jagger could turn towards Flash or he could proceed on a direct course to Leek by descending to a ford at Dun Cow's Grove (the lower part of this steep descent is deeply hollowed) and continuing up what is now a narrow, but tarmac'd, lane leading to the high ground between Morridge Top and Morridge End. Until 1765, or a little later, the present Leek-Buxton road (p173) had not been made, and the packhorse way continued in its southwesterly direction over the ridge uninterrupted. The way descended past Downsdale Farm (028654) and the present hollowed lane to what was a crossing-of-the-ways just north of Gib Tor; the north-south way was the old route from Buxton to Leek (p174).

But we must return to Washgate and examine the likely destinations of jaggers following this way in the opposite direction. The steep ascent from Washgate into Derbyshire affords a good example of a paved packhorse way; it led through Leycote to Booth (058680) where it was crossed by the way from Hollinsclough (p93). From Booth the way ahead would seem to have forked, one route climbing over High Edge and Harpur Hill to Buxton, the other passing round the southern end of High Edge and across the head of Dowel Dale north of Greensides Farm, where a footpath and wall form a parish boundary. On the west side of Hind Low is Harley Cross Gate (077689); Harley Farm, about half-a-mile south-east, was recorded in 1382. The Hind Low area has for many years been so extensively quarried that the way eastwards from Harley Cross Gate can now be only conjectured; it was probably towards Chelmorton.

5.7 Flash and Three Shire Heads

Standing 1,525ft above sea level, Flash claims to be the highest village in England. The land is poor and the smallholdings have always been inadequate to support a family in any comfort. Two centuries ago many of the men were pedlars and only part-time farmers, their trade being mainly in silk, mohair and twist buttons from Macclesfield; the route would be up Ridgehill past the old guidestone (956692) variously known as Saxon Cross or Greenway Cross; the bridge over the Highmoor Brook just below is Greenway Bridge and the length of road between the two was the Greenway. From there the track forded the Clough

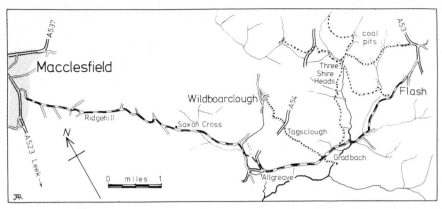

Map 31 Packhorse ways to Flash and Three Shire Heads.

38 Four packhorse ways meet at Three Shire Heads; as can be seen beneath the arch, the bridge has at some date been widened.

39 Two of the track-ways converging on the bridge at Three Shire Heads.

Brook and can be followed as a footpath to Allgreave, then as the present road to Flash. The Flash pedlars were known locally as 'fudge-mounters'; they travelled the country with their packs 'kippering and twanning' as they went, that is, sleeping in barns and begging their food. They got a bad name, but not all of them merited Samuel Smiles' description 'wild and half-barbarous'; the pedlar John Lomas (1747-1823), for example, built the Methodist Chapel at Hollinsclough (065665) and his initials can be seen on a tablet above the entrance.

Rather more than a mile north-west of Flash, Cheshire, Derbyshire and Staffordshire meet at Three Shire Heads (009685). On Speed's map of 1610 this is 'Three Shire Stones' and three tall stones are depicted, one in each county. Of these stones there is now no trace, but a packhorse bridge, probably there when Speed drew his map, still spans the infant River Dane just above Panniers Pool. This name was first recorded in 1533; perhaps at that time there was no bridge and the horses with their panniers had to ford the small rock pool. At the bridge, which has at some time been widened by three feet on the upstream side, four pack-horse ways converge; they led in various directions from Cheshire and Staffordshire into Derbyshire, forming a network of narrow tracks, often between walls, which can readily be followed on the 2½ inch OS map (Sheet SK 06) and which make ideal routes for walkers.

5.8 Gradbach to Wildboarclough

One of the ways from Three Shire Heads follows the River Dane down to Gradbach (994659) where there was a mill as far back as 1640. The present mill was built in 1785 by Thomas Dakeyne of Darley Dale; the waterwheel has gone, but those who do not remember it can judge its unusual size from the depth and height of the wheelhousing at the south end of the building. The mill was first used to spin flax, but in the middle of the last century this was changed to waste-silk spinning, 200 being employed. Finally, according to local tradition, Gradbach Mill made carpets, working in association with a mill at Wildboarclough (982686); materials were carried between the mills by packhorses and the way they went makes a very pleasant walk. From Gradbach Mill a modern footbridge crosses the Dane and leads immediately to a typical narrow packhorse way. This is very steep and it is not surprising to find a series of stone horse-troughs at the halfway point to the Allgreave road; arrived at the road, the man leading the train could himself have slaked his thirst at the Eagle and Child. This eighteenth-century house ceased to be an inn around 1920 but kept its old name, a badge of the Stanley family, showing that it once belonged to Lord Derby, who still owns Crag Hall over the hill at Wildboarclough. The packhorse way continues uphill by

40 Packhorse way from Gradbach Mill (now converted to a Youth Hostel) leading to other mills at Wildboarclough.

41 The Eagle and Child, formerly an inn, at the crossing of the Macclesfield-Flash and the Gradbach-Wildboarclough pack-horse routes.

the east side of the Eagle and Child, descends to cross the A54, passes by Tagsclough farm-buildings (985679) and then becomes a footpath to the top corner of Berrybank Wood. Down the further edge of the wood it again assumes the character of a packhorse way before finally degenerating to a footpath leading to Wildboarclough.

5.9 Jaggers Gate

From the packhorse bridge at Three Shire Heads, one way leads northeast and passes over Axe Edge Moor towards Buxton. A packhorse way from Buxton west towards Macclesfield is recorded as far back as 1600 in a manuscript by Anthony Bradshaw of Duffield, describing 'The Bounds, Extremities and Meres of the High Peak Forest'. From a point below Tideswell, the southern boundary of this hunting forest was defined as 'ffollowing Wye to Wyehead: ffrom Wyehead ffollowing Jaggers Gate to Goyte Water'. The course of the River Wye in this upstream direction is through Chee Dale and Ashwood Dale to Buxton, where it is a feature of the Pavilion Gardens and Serpentine Walks, and so to the several springs among the high hills west of Burbage. The Jaggers Gate linking the headwaters of the Wye and Goyt must have been the old road from Burbage (044728) to the Cat and Fiddle (001719); once clear of the houses beyond Burbage, this is now a rough track as far as the head of the Goyt Valley (017716), where there is now a carpark with metalled roads up to the Cat and Fiddle and down the beautiful Goyt Valley itself. About a mile down this valley the packhorse bridge that formerly spanned the stream at Goyt's Bridge has been re-erected; as originally sited, this bridge was on a saltway (p122).

5.10 Chapel en le Frith, Hayfield and Glossop

Many packhorse ways from Lancashire and Cheshire crossed the hills between Glossop and Chapel en le Frith, and we know that in the eighteenth century Squire Frith, who lived at Bank Hall (052788) amassed a fortune from his trains of packhorses; there was at Chapel a field called Carriers' Meadow where, presumably, carriers could graze their horses overnight at a small charge. To the east of Chapel a way formerly known as the Packhorse Road winds north-west from Tideswell through Peak Forest, up Perry Dale (105808), past Rushup, across Roych Clough, and so by Mount Famine (055847) to Hayfield, where there is a Packhorse Inn. From Rushup, much of this very old way still runs between walls, finally descending by an excellent length of hollow-way to Highgate and so into Hayfield itself; the way is indeed a high 'gate', climbing to 1,450 ft between South Head and Mount Famine. There was also much traffic from Hayfield to the north; the woollen mills in Hayfield at one time sent their wool by packhorse through Glossop and over Holme Moss to Holmfirth, a distance of 15 miles, to have it dyed.

The medieval way already noted (p59) from Hayfield past Edale Cross into the Vale of Edale was used by packhorses into the eighteenth century. Leaving Hayfield on the north side of the Royal Hotel, the way first follows the road leading to Kinder Reservoir but, after a mile, turns south to Coldwell Clough (055858) before again changing direction to climb due east. The way passes between stone gate posts and then continues between walls. For much of its length the way has become hollowed by centuries of use; it crosses the Oaken Clough Brook at Stony Ford and part of the final ascent to Edale Cross (077861) is roughly metalled. Eastwards from the Cross the way is again hollow for a short

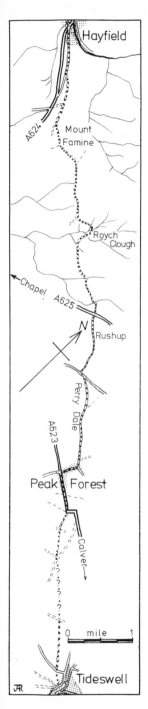

Map 32   Packhorse route from Hayfield to Tideswell.

42   Packhorse bridge at the foot of Jacob's Ladder leading to Edale Head (*Painting by W. B. Gardner, 1908*)

43   A packhorse way worn to the bedrock; the guide-post marks the junction of Chapel Gate with the Rushup Edge route.

distance and there is another paved section before the steepening descent towards Jacob's Ladder and the fine packhorse bridge, only 27 in between parapets, over the River Noe. Packhorses did not attempt the precipitous direct descent to the bridge; the packhorse way follows a gentle rake to the south then bends sharply to come between walls past the ruins of Edale Head House. There is paving between the walls, and in the elbow of the bend there is an enclosure that may have been for the overnight grazing of packhorses while the jaggers slept in some outbuilding of Edale Head House.

Further north, from Glossop, the Roman road that became known as Doctor's Gate (p38), leading to the Woodlands Valley, was used by packhorses until the turnpike road was constructed (p150).

5.11 Around Castleton and Edale

A dramatic approach to Castleton is along the old route from Tideswell, consistently above the 1000 ft contour until within a mile of Castleton, when it plunges 400 ft into the centre of the village. This steep descent is 'Siggate' on the modern OS map but 'Side Gate' on the original 1840 edition; the name presumably means the 'gate', or way, up the side of the hill.

From Castleton a way known as Hollowford Road leads north-west in a straight line over the ridge to Edale. As the road leaves Castleton there is a stream on the left running in a deep hollow, and one may assume that at one time this stream was crossed, in the hollow, through a ford; this Hollowford is in fact recorded as far back as 1455. For some distance Hollowford Road is now tarmac'd, but as it begins the steep ascent it narrows to a bridle way up another deeply worn hollow to reach the open hillside where it is crossed by a track that passes by Mam Farm and Woodseat and leads to Only Grange. From the crossing, the Edale way is for some distance roughly paved with stones set on edge, the more stable setting on a gradient; higher up, across a more level boggy section, stones are set flat. The ridge is attained at Hollins Cross, where there is an orientation table erected to the memory of Tom Hyett of Long Eaton by his fellow ramblers. The way descends north-west to Edale via Hollins Farm, but to the north-east there is another hollowed way down to Backtor Farm and Backtor Bridge across the River Noe.

We have already suggested (p12) that a prehistoric trackway led along Rushup Edge to Mam Tor and beyond. There is clear evidence on the ground that many centuries later this ridge-way was used by packhorse trains. The route may be followed from the point (092825) at which the Tideswell-Hayfield packhorse way (p98) crosses the Chapel en le Frith to Castleton turnpike (p149). A way that is in places worn to

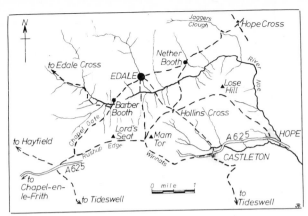

Map 33 Some packhorse ways around Castleton and Edale.

44 Hope Cross, a restored medieval landmark.

the bedrock, climbs the edge and in about half a mile, at an altitude of 1,600 ft , reaches the point from which Chapel Gate branches north into the Vale of Edale. The packhorse way along Rushup Edge lies in a worn hollow along its southern flank; anyone walking here when the wind is from the north, will understand why the jaggers kept to a line just below the exposed ridge top. Their way thus passed a little below the unusually large Bronze Age burial mound on Lord's Seat (1,800 ft) and kept on the warmer side of the ridge before curving round to Mam Nick, from where one hollow-way descends via Greenlands to Edale. The more important way from Mam Nick would continue along the ridge, but the southern flank of Mam Tor is both loose and precipitous; jaggers wishing to pursue their high-level route were therefore forced at this point to move round to the north flank of the ridge, and the way that their packhorses trod and slowly hollowed is very plain. Once past the ramparts of the Iron Age fort, the way follows the ridge to Hollins Cross and eventually descends from the southern flank of Lose Hill through Lose Hill Farm and by what is now a footpath to a former crossroads on the west side of Hope church; the lower part of this way from Hollins Cross is marked 'Edale Road' on the 1819 Enclosure Map for Hope Parish.

Chapel Gate leaves the Vale of Edale at Barber Booth, crossing gently sloping fields near the Manor House before slanting up the steep hillside; in places it is so deeply hollowed that it has become founderous. This old

101

way aims directly over the west end of Rushup Edge towards Chapel en le Frith, which is the Chapel to which this 'gate' led.

Edale, sited in a shallow and fertile valley and mentioned in Domesday Book, was evidently at one time a place of some importance as five packhorse ways converge there (the way from Barber Booth serving the traffic both from Edale Cross and from Chapel Gate). The way eastwards from the village crossed Grindsbrook by the narrow packhorse bridge and can be followed as a footpath to Nether Booth, which is on Saxton's map of 1577. Most of these 'booths' along the Vale of Edale were recorded in sixteenth- or seventeenth-century documents; they were simple shelters for cattle and sheep, and for the herdsmen and shepherds who tended them. From Nether Booth the way eastwards continued past Clough Farm and across Jaggers Clough to Hope Cross (161874), a medieval landmark that has been restored; it now stands nearly 8 ft high and the squared capstone reads: Shefield; Hope; Edale; Glossop, 1737.

We have left until the last what was presumably the most used route through Castleton — that down the Winnats and on to Hope; in addition to the usual range of merchandise, salt was carried along this route and it is treated in more detail under Saltways (p121).

5.12 Howden Moors and Derwent Moors

Below Howden Moor, the River Derwent was formerly crossed by a ford at Slippery Stones (169952). There is now a packhorse bridge, but this was brought from Derwent village (185886) before the area became submerged by Ladybower Reservoir; the bridge was re-erected at Slippery Stones in 1959 as a memorial to John Derry, who loved these high moors and fought for access to them. From Slippery Stones there is a way to Penistone known as Cut Gate; it was a packhorse route from Woodlands Valley to Penistone. In confirmation of this there is an old fingerpost at 164891; its arms point to 'Glossop' and to 'Birchinlee and Penistone'; the descent to the Woodlands Valley, and thence to Glossop, would be past Rowlee Farm. There is a good length of hill-road paved with small stones set on edge just by the guidepost, and the way here is

Map 34   Cut Gate leading to Penistone.

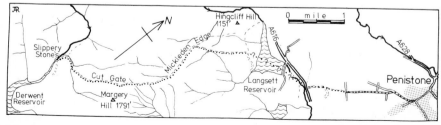

quite deeply hollowed. Cut Gate led to Penistone market and light carts may also have used it since it is referred to as 'Cart Gate' in a document of 1571. From Slippery Stones, the way climbed the northern shoulder of Margery Hill (189957), reaching a height above 1,700 feet before turning more to the north along Mickleden Edge; this way over the peat is sometimes called 'Black Dike', but is nevertheless part of Cut Gate. The way then passes to the east of Hingcliff Hill (195999) aiming directly for Penistone, but is now interrupted in the valley bottom by Langsett Reservoir. This way to Penistone market was still being followed within living memory and was kept in repair by the farmers who used it.

The packhorse bridge at Derwent, which we have just mentioned, was built in the Middle Ages and was repaired in 1682. It lay on 'the common way which leads from Sheffield towards Darwent', to quote a fourteenth-century charter. Leaving Sheffield via Stannington, the packhorses kept to the ridge north of the Rivelin valley; once the climb out of Stannington had been achieved, the way was reasonably level as far as Moscar Cross, a guidestone (231884). In 1571 this was recorded as Humblestone Cross, but the present name was already coming into use by the mid-seventeenth century; in those days a medieval cross presumably stood here as a landmark. The present guidestone, set up to comply with the Act of Parliament of 1702, is inscribed on its four faces: Sheffeild Road; Hathersage; Hope Roa[d]; Bradfield. The first half-mile of the way to Hope can be seen over the wall behind the guidestone; it leads past a small pinewood to Cutthroat Bridge. From there the old way has been obliterated by the modern roads and reservoir, but can be resumed at Yorkshire Bridge; this bridge on the way from Hope to Sheffield and so into Yorkshire, was first recorded in 1599.

Returning now to Cutthroat Bridge, the 'common way which leads from Sheffield to Darwent' proceeded almost due west from near the bridge to pass below Hurkling Stones and Whinstone Lee Tor before turning north for the final descent to Derwent village. The Hathersage way from Moscar Cross is for a short distance lost beneath the modern drive to Moscar Lodge, dated 1872, but from the main road a footpath leads south to a very clear hollow-way leading to the northern end of Stanage Edge; however, the Hathersage way soon rakes to pass beneath Stanage End, making for Moscar Stones (220854) and thence to Hathersage.

5.13 Bamford Moor, Hallam Moors and Eastmoor

J. Radley has been able to trace over sixty packhorse ways over these moors, which, except for the cutting of a few turnpike roads, have changed little since packhorse trains crossed them in so many directions,

Map 35   Packhorse ways from the Woodlands Valley to Sheffield.

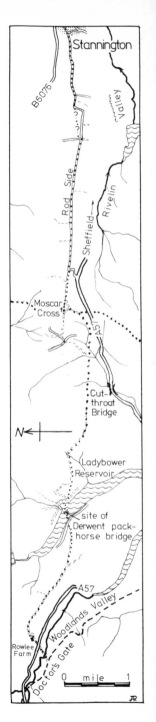

45   The medieval Derwent Bridge before the village was submerged by Ladybower Reservoir; the bridge has been rebuilt at Slippery Stones.

46   Hollow Gate, fording Burbage Brook on its way over Millstone Edge to Leadmill Bridge, Hathersage.

but chiefly towards or from Sheffield and Chesterfield.

An important focus for the ways over the Hallam Moors was the guidepost set up long ago at Stanedge Pole (247844). There was a pole here, on the edge of the moor at a height of 1,453ft, at least as early as 1550; many initials have been cut into the rock supporting the pole, but four sets can be distinguished as those of parish road surveyors who renewed the pole, every fifty years or so: T.C. 1550, H.W. 1581, T.M. 1631, H.H. 1697, F.N. 1740. The way to the pole out of Sheffield was via Lydgate and the Long Causeway, and the pole guided jaggers to an all-important way down the precipitous barrier of Stanage Edge. The long, gently sloping, track leading north-west and passing above the Buck Stone (231847) before turning south to join the metalled road at the corner of a plantation (227844), is probably a more recent trackway for the transport of millstones; a particularly large millstone lies by the side of this track just north of the Buck Stone. The old packhorse way from Stanedge Pole dropped very steeply over the Edge on a narrow paved way leading due south. The Roman road (p38) which descended from Stanage Edge a half mile north-west was also later used by pack-horses, and the jaggers may have had some sort of shelter at the Buck Stone, which has two squared sockets for roof timbers and around which there is a walled enclosure.

One way off the moors was via Bole Hill, Bamford and Lydgate to Yorkshire Bridge (198850); in the seventeenth century this was a wooden horsebridge, but it was replaced by a stone bridge in 1695. Another way, perhaps the most used, was to Hathersage where there is a Jaggers Lane. The Scotsman's Pack at Hathersage is an inn name suggesting that the Scottish packmen, who travelled throughout England in the sixteenth and seventeenth centuries, were often seen in this part of

Map 36   Packhorse ways near Hathersage.

Derbyshire. Turning up to Camp Green from the Scotsman's Pack, a farm road leads to Carhead; beyond a cattle-grid a packhorse hollow-way climbs to Toothill Farm and by Overstones Farm into the old way to Ringinglow.

Below Hathersage the River Derwent was crossed at Hazelford (234-806); this was on an important trade-route, Halifax Gate, for the carrying of wool and woollen goods to and from Halifax and other Yorkshire woollen centres. The ford was impassable on many days in the year and in 1708 application was made at the Quarter Sessions for the building of a bridge; the sum of £20 allowed for this purpose proved to be inadequate and the following year the grant was raised to £50 for 'a wooden bridge with two stone piers and stone abutments'. However, a flood washed everything away before the bridge was even completed. Quarter Sessions then decided to build a bridge of three stone arches and this was done, only for it to be found 'insufficient to receive the water in a large flood'.

The Derwent drains a wide area of moorland and to cope with so much water an extra arch was added at each end of the bridge together with causeways, bringing the total cost to £166. Hazelford Bridge has for long been known as Leadmill Bridge and the original stone arches were widened both upstream and down in 1928.

East of Leadmill Bridge a packhorse way climbed over Millstone Edge; it can be picked up by following the Sheffield road (A625) from Hathersage. Not far short of the corner of Millstone Edge known as 'The Surprise', from the sudden panorama as one rounds the bend from the opposite direction, a track leads back to a disused quarry; three millstones from this quarry can be seen in the retaining wall to the quarry track, and from near these millstones the packhorse way climbs over the Edge. From the top it can be followed as a hollow-way to a car park by the side of the Sheffield road. Ignore the footpath opposite the car park — the packhorse way followed the line of the present road for about 100 yards before bearing south-east as a fine hollow-way leading to a ford through Burbage Brook. This part of the packhorse way is appropriately known as Hollow Gate; it led to Chesterfield by way of Frogatt Pole (268789) and Lady's Cross (277781); this Cross is mentioned in a document of 1263 and is said to have served as a marker for the junction of the boundaries of Hathersage, Holmesfield and Totley, although this junction actually lies some distance to the south-west. Along the way from Lady's Cross to Chesterfield there are two more guide-crosses to the north of Bole Hill (296747). From the last cross (295748), which stands near the top end of, and within, a conifer plantation, the packhorse trains would turn more to the east to come, in half-a-dozen miles, to Chesterfield. This last cross, which offers a good example of how a medieval

47 (*left*) Guidestone at Curbar Gap, where several packhorse ways meet.

48 (*below*) Clapper bridge across the Bar Brook near the Baslow-Sheffield road.

cross was set in a stone base, also served as a guide to jaggers coming over the moors past Swine Sty (271750) to Curbar Gap (260747), where there is a guidestone inscribed: Shefield Rd; Dronfield Road; Chesterfeild Road; Tidswall Road; Humphery Gregory, Supervisor 1709. The Quarter Sessions Order Book for 1709, from which we quoted earlier in this chapter, laid down severe penalties for further neglect of Parliament's directive of 1702 to erect guidestones; perhaps Humphrey Gregory, by adding his name and date to this guidestone intended to show that he, at least, was carrying out his instructions.

The packhorse way from Curbar Gap to Chesterfield was turnpiked in 1759 (p161) and straightened to the present line of tarmac'd road. About 100yd north of the point where this road crosses the A621, the rather insignificant Bar Brook is spanned by a fine clapper bridge consisting of two stone slabs, each about 9ft long; one bears the date 1777 preceded by the letter 'H' in reference to a perambulation of the Holmesfield boundary in that year, but there is also the date 1742 on the top of the same slab.

The 'Tidswall' way sets out from the Curbar Gap guidestone down the steep road to Calver Bridge and thence through Stoney Middleton. But there are other old ways from Curbar Gap not indicated on the guidestone. One of these branches from the road to Calver Bridge and leads to Stanton Ford (248735) and Hassop; most of the way to the ford is a parish boundary, but not all of its length is a right-of-way. It passes the Cundy Graves (255744), five rough stone slabs laid flat in a small hollow; they bear the initials of Thomas Cundy, of nearby Grislowfields Farm, his wife Ada, and their children Olive, Nellie and Thomas, who all died of the plague in 1632. A modern inscription alongside points out that this was 34 years before the outbreak of plague in Eyam. Between this burial ground and Baslow Edge, which frowns above, a bridle-way slants down from near Curbar Gap to join Baslow Bar for its final steep descent into Baslow. Referring to the word 'Bar', an early writer explained that 'In the Peak of Derbyshire all those steep and precipitous roads which run down from the cliffs to the valleys, where the villages generally are placed, they call Bars'. In the Over End part of Baslow, Bar Road has every appearance of an ordinary road climbing gently between modern houses; after a few hundred yards, however, its original character becomes plain — a steep packhorse way, centuries old. Just beyond the junction (258728) with the bridle-way from Curbar Gap, Baslow Bar makes a double bend, and here is a water-trough for the horses; towards the top of the Bar there is a length of rough paving. Arrived at Wellington's Monument, the way levels over Eaglestone Flat and passes a guidestone (275740) that is unusual in being inscribed on one face only: Chesterfeild Roade.

South of this way to Chesterfield lies Brampton East Moor, the high ground that provides water for the fountains and cascades in the gardens of Chatsworth House. On the moor is the prehistoric burial mound known as Hob Hurst's House (287692), which seems to have served as a focus for packhorse ways. One of these leads due east to a crossroads at Longside Moor (311688) and thence through Holymoorside to Chesterfield. Another leads north past an old guidestone (288697): Bakewell Road; Chesterfield Road. The packhorse way to Bakewell led via Park Farm (273692) to Mill Bridge, which spanned the Derwent near Chatsworth Mill (259688); this bridge was demolished when Beeley Bridge ('One Arch Bridge') was built in 1761. Another packhorse way from the Park Farm area can readily be traced as a deep hollow-way leading down to Beeley Hilltop (270685); it is now used as a footpath which continues down the fields to Beeley village.

Further south there were important crossings of the River Derwent at Rowsley (257658) and at Darley Bridge (271621). The bridge at Rowsley was repaired in 1682 and has since been widened. The way from it over

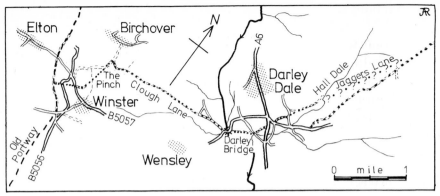

Map 37   Packhorse ways near Darley Bridge.

Fallinge Edge to the east was originally a packhorse way to Chesterfield, passing by Gladwin's Mark (305667), a name suggesting an ancient markstone at nearby crossroads.

Darley Bridge still has two of the original pointed arches, both ribbed; three other arches were rebuilt in the later semicircular style when widening was carried out on the upstream side. A reference to this bridge in 1682 mentioned seven arches, so two other arches may be hidden beneath the present approaches. Not far to the north of the bridge is Four Lane Ends; the road to the left leads to Churchtown and is now known as Church Lane, but at least as far back as 1635 it was Ghost Lane. The ghost was that of a Scottish pedlar who was robbed and murdered there.

From the east end of Darley Bridge a footpath leads directly to Warney Bridge, and a lane then takes up the line to Ryecroft and so into Hall Dale. During the reign of Elizabeth I the Old Hall (demolished in 1771) was owned by Roger Columbell; a map that once belonged to this Roger shows his sheep walks and marks Jaggers Lane, following the general direction of Hall Dale. However, an alternative packhorse route from Darley Dale up to Beeley Moor followed the opposite (eastern) side of Hall Dale. It can be followed as a green lane branching north-east from the present road (the Two Dales Turnpike, p156) and soon passes an early eighteenth-century guidestone now serving as a gatepost (285635); it bears a single inscription: Chasterfield Road, with a pointing hand. Beyond Victoria Cottages this Back Lane, as it is now called, is metalled and climbs steadily, passing Moor Farm, at one time an inn — The Quiet Woman — and leading into Flash Lane. On Beeley Moor another guidestone stands (296674) just off the present road, but hollow-ways lead to it; the four faces are inscribed: Offerton (ie Alfreton); Chesterfeild; Chatsworth; Bakewell.

On the west side of Darley Bridge the lane to Stanton Lees soon forks; to the left is Oldfield Lane, leading over the southern shoulder of Cowley Knowl (256619) into Clough Lane. This is a packhorse way and some sections are paved with gritstone slabs; this route is likely to have been used for the transport of ore from lead mines in the area. Clough Lane terminates at Upper Town (240616) where some old stocks stand by the roadside. Turning south, the narrow road soon becomes a deep hollow-way known as 'The Pinch'; this formerly led straight across the valley bottom into the disused lane that crosses the B5057, passing by the new Winster burial ground and then crossing the B5056 to join the Old Portway.

5.14 Between the Derwent and the Wye

The major north to south route on the eastern side of the Peak District was the Old Portway (p49), which forded the River Wye at Ashford. It is recorded that towards the end of the seventeenth century, 300 packhorses laden with malt from the Derby area passed through Ashford each week. In addition to this ancient route, a way led from the same ford through Great Longstone to a gap (205732) in Longstone Edge, beyond which it followed Black Harry Lane into Middleton Dale and so up to Eyam. In Eyam there are two interesting street names: Lydgate, leading into Mill Lane and so down to Stoney Middleton; Causeway, leading into an old way past Riley Graves and down to the Derwent valley. Lydgate was at one time the principal way into the village and a watchman was posted at the gate every night.

Northwards from Eyam, as a continuation of the way up Eyam Dale, Water Lane climbs very steeply to join the metalled road that passes Mompesson's Well on its way to Moor End (224780) on Sir William Road (p164). Northwards again from Moor End four tracks radiate over

49   Lydgate at Eyam, leading to Stoney Middleton.

the moor, but one of these peters out and another leads only to a quarry. The track to the north-east was a packhorse route to Hathersage. From the stile on Sir William Road the way at first follows a fence and the landmark to aim at is Millstone Edge; the path becomes hollowed as it approaches two gateposts in a tumbled wall (a parish boundary), beyond which it turns north to aim straight for Hathersage Church. This old way over Eyam Moor joins a by-road at Leam, but where this road takes a long double-bend to descend the steep hill to Hazelford Hall, the old way kept straight ahead — as does a footpath; three packhorse hollow-ways can readily be traced on the hillside. From Hazelford Hall the way crossed the Derwent at Leadmill Bridge and so arrived in Hathersage.

The way from Eyam and then over Eyam Moor to the north-west led into the bottom of Bretton Clough and through Abney (198799) to Robin Hood's Cross (184803). Only the cross-base remains and even this is built into the bottom of a wall. The cross originally marked the junction of the parishes of Abney, Hazelbadge and Bradwell and is referred to in 1317; the old name was Robin Cross, probably so called after Robert (or Robin) Archer, who was Lord of Abney at that time. From the site of this ancient landmark a fine example of a deeply hollowed packhorse way with relics of paving descends from Bradwell Edge into Bradwell village; towards the top of this hollow-way there was a resting place for the horses with a spring, now dry, in one corner.

In addition to the way from Ashford over Longstone Edge to Eyam, many other packhorse ways crossed these lonely moors, and in the early eighteenth century the trains were frequently attacked and robbed by a highwayman who took the name Black Harry — Black Harry House (203745) stands a third of a mile west of Black Harry Lane. He was eventually caught, and was hanged and then gibbeted at Wardlow Mires (181756); an account is preserved at the Bull's Head in Wardlow village.

On the whole, travelling may have been safer in the preceding century when Thomas Hobbes, gathering material for his *Wonders of the Peak*, rode over Longstone Edge on his way from Chatsworth to Castleton. He describes how he followed a 'rugged track' used by packhorses; it led through Pilsley (241710) and across the valley to Hassop. This old way, now somewhat overgrown, can be followed on foot. From Pilsley it first leads west to a T-junction; the way south climbs via Handley Lane to Bakewell, while to the right a narrow green lane, between walls, develops into a very deep hollow-way as it changes direction to descend to the A619, which, along this length, is known as 'Thirteen Bends'. The packhorse way went straight across this road but the footpath lies a short distance east; it leads through a wood to cross the Rymas Brook by a clapper bridge worth preserving and then again comes between walls to climb to Hassop. The old way has for long been

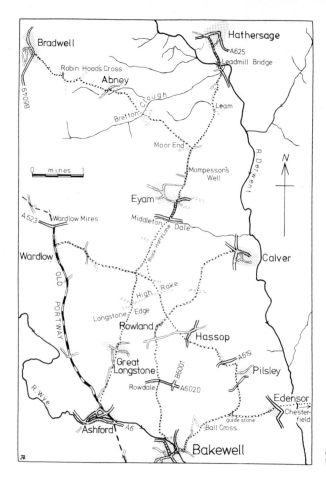

Map 38   Packhorse ways between the Derwent and the Wye.

50   Guidestone, dated 1709, at Ball Cross on the old road from Bakewell to Edensor.

interrupted by the parkland of Hassop Hall; originally, having climbed from the brook it kept straight on to the line of trees west of Torrs Farm (220724), following this line north-north-west up the hill to join Wigley Lane. It can be plainly seen north-east of the reservoir 50 yd from Wigley Lane, which was followed onto High Rake and so across to Wardlow or to Eyam.

5.15 Around Bakewell

At the north end of Bakewell there is a notable packhorse bridge, Holme Bridge, dating from 1664 and having five segmental and two semi-circular arches. Directly opposite the north end of this bridge a lane ascends past a stone quarry and, arrived at the top of Holme Bank,

51 Holme Bridge, Bakewell, dates from 1664.

continues between walls; this was an important packhorse way. It
crosses the Ashford-Baslow turnpike at Rowdale tollhouse (214709);
the siting of this tollhouse would suggest that cross traffic of packhorses
was still considerable in turnpike days. From the turnpike the packhorse
way climbed the field to the north and can be followed as a footpath
which continues north alongside the high wall of Hassop Park; this wall
was evidently built to take in most of half-a-mile of the old way, as can
be seen where the footpath eventually turns through a stile to rejoin the
original line as a green lane. This makes a cross-road with the turnpike
from Hassop to Little Longstone where, incidentally, there is a Packhorse Inn. From Rowland (214725) the packhorse trains could head for
Wardlow, Eyam or Calver.

To the east of Bakewell, beyond the bridge, a road climbs round the
southern and eastern sides of Castle Hill then crosses the old railway; in
about 100yd, where the road bends slightly left, the packhorse way to
Sheffield and Chesterfield keeps straight ahead through the hillside
woods to Ball Cross. On its steepest part alternative hollow-ways can be
seen on the right of the path. The way was formerly paved: '1678 — Pd.
Ottewell Broomhead for Causing the Bawcross…£3.19.8'. The tarmac'd road that slants up the hillside on an easier gradient to Ball Cross
was constructed in 1810; the ancient causeway that climbed directly
through the woods was taken up, broken, and used in making the new
road. The base of Ball Cross itself escaped destruction at that time but
has since disappeared. Half-a-mile beyond the crest of the hill the road
divides and at the fork there is a guidestone (Sheffield Rode; Chesterfield; Bakewell Rode 1709); to the left leads down Handley Lane to

Pilsley and on to Sheffield, to the right leads to Edensor. This village was moved from near Chatsworth House to its present site in 1839; it was laid out by Sir Joseph Paxton and the scheme was completed thirty years later by Sir Gilbert Scott's new church. The old way forward to Chesterfield has already been described (p108).

West of Bakewell, packhorse trains would use the Old Portway (p49) leading over Haddon Fields to Alport; a cross-track led from Nether Haddon (the village that was adjacent to Haddon Hall but that was abandoned in the early fifteenth century) to Coalpit Bridge (214652), so named because packhorses carried coal this way from pits around Chesterfield. According to the 1840 OS map, the point (218653) at which this track crossed the Old Portway was known as Two Trees — evidently at one time a landmark; the name is now applied to the point (216662) at which the Old Portway joins the road leading from Conksbury to Bakewell. The packhorse trains carrying malt, which we have already met with at Ashford, came along the Old Portway and in 1718 a complaint was presented to the Derbyshire Sessions on the urgent need for a bridge at Alport:

> Great gangs of London carriers as well as drifts of malt-horses and other carriers and passengers goe this ancient waye, which lies in a hollow frequently overflowed by the swollen stream. Heavy rains have so scoured out the channel as to render the ford impassable for as long as 8 or 10 days, whilst at all times carriers with loaden horses and passengers cannot pass the saide road without great danger of being cast away.

As a result of this complaint, the 1718 Sessions directed that a horsebridge be built; considerably later, as we shall see, this was replaced by a bridge wide enough for coaches and waggons (Fig 5). The stone footbridge a hundred yards upstream was built as a private entrance to Monk's Hall; the bridge carrying the present main road across the River Lathkill dates from about 1800. This road formerly crossed the River Wye by the old Fillyford Bridge (241659), which can be seen by looking over the upstream parapet of the modern bridge. When excavating for road improvements here in about 1935, a length of old road, kerbed and metalled, was uncovered; its orientation indicated that it would have forded the river at a point — the original Filly Ford — some ten yards from the old bridge.

5.16 Matlock, Cromford and Wirksworth

Matlock Bridge was referred to in clerk's Latin — *Pontem de Matelock* — in the mid-thirteenth century; it has several times been rebuilt. On the downstream side the present structure has four pointed arches, probably dating from the fifteenth century; it was originally a narrow packhorse

52   The old Matlock Bridge in 1802. (Britton & Brayley: *Beauties of England and Wales*)

bridge and this was revealed, still in good condition, when the bridge was widened and largely rebuilt early in the present century. Matlock Bridge is a meeting-of-the-ways and has evidently been an important crossing of the River Derwent from medieval times. A traveller coming this way in the eighteenth century wrote:

> The road from Buxton to Matlock is over naked hills and deserted dales; nothing worthy of notice occurred except the vast number of packhorses travelling, of which we counted sixty in a drove; their chief loading is wool and malt, which they carry from Nottingham and Derby to Manchester.

As we have already seen, Hereward Street (p24), although coming north from Cromford over the high ground east of the river, then ascended Matlock Bank along what is now A632. We may therefore assume that, from the time in the thirteenth century when Matlock Bridge became available, a way would climb east from the bridge to join the old Roman Road. Three miles forward, at Ashover (348630), there is a Jaggers Lane, while rather nearer to the south-east is the village of Holloway (326563); both names indicate former packhorse ways.

From the western end of Matlock Bridge a packhorse way leads to Grangemill; it runs from Matlock Bridge in a virtually straight line of linking lanes — Salters Lane (p125), Nailor Lane, Moorlands Lane (Morelandes Yate in 1543), Blakemere Lane. But the network of old ways on Bonsall Moor is confused by former access roads to lead mines. The rules for setting out these access ways were based on the Inquisition for the King's Field of the High Peak held in Ashbourne in 1288; even these ancient rules were based on still earlier usage. When a lead miner found a new vein and had registered his discovery with the Barmaster,

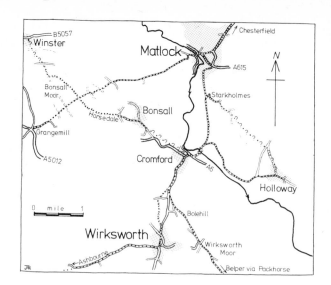

Map 39   Packhorse
ways around Matlock
and Wirksworth.

he had the right of access to the nearest highway, but for horse transport
only, not for 'wayn or sled' except by agreement; the width of this mine
road was usually decided by the Barmaster and two jurymen of the
Barmote Court walking abreast with arms outstretched and fingers
touching. On Bonsall Moor, to help us to disentangle packhorse
through-ways from mere access ways, there are two early eighteenth-
century guidestones. The more interesting of these, marked GS(1) on
Map 40 and located at 244594, lies on a packhorse way that forks from
the Old Portway near Shothouse Spring, about a mile north of
Grangemill; this old way still marks a parish boundary. Inscriptions on
the four faces of this guidestone read: 'Matlock; Ashborn; Bakewel;
Chesterfeild; 1757 Near this place lieth....' The end of this 1757
addition is illegible, but a former lead miner of Wirksworth has told us
that, when a young man, he made a rubbing and could then read 'Near
this place lieth Alsop of Slaley', a hamlet near Bonsall. This Alsop was
evidently a suicide, and had forfeited his right to churchyard burial; for
such as him, burial at a cross-roads was once common, the two roads
above his mortal remains forming the cross that would be his only hope
of future salvation. For the people of Bonsall this particular cross-roads
would have the advantage of being on their parish boundary; the burial
would most probably be on the west side of the guidestone and so outside
their parish. The four ways indicated on the guidestone would be: to
Matlock along a way that has since disappeared but which presumably
joined Salter's Lane; to Ashbourne via Grangemill, and, as the turnpike
(p180) had not then been made, probably continuing through Aldwark
and Brassington; to Bakewell along the Old Portway; to Chesterfield

116

Map 40   Bonsall Moor and its two guidestones; GS2 is shown in its probable original position.

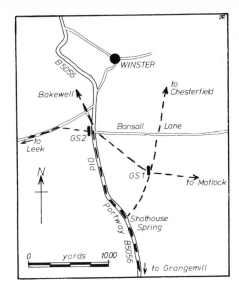

53   Cromford Bridge with fifteenth-century arches on the downstream side; the other side has later rounded arches.

via Darley Bridge. Guidestone 2 is now used as a gatepost on the west side of B5056 at 238597; it is likely to have been moved from a cross-roads a little to the north, as shown on Map 40. Its faces indicate the ways to: Bakewell; Bonsall; Worksworth; Leeke. The way north to Bakewell and south to Wirksworth would be along the Old Portway; to Bonsall along Bonsall Lane; to Leek via Pikehall, Green Lane, Biggin and Hartington. Also crossing Bonsall Moor would be a direct way from Bonsall to Winster via Horsedale (Map 39).

Cromford Bridge was mentioned by Leland in the reign of Henry VIII; the bridge that he saw may well be incorporated in the present structure, the three arches on the downstream side being of fifteenth-century style. The remains of the bridge chapel also have features of this period. In Leland's time, and for long afterwards, Cromford Bridge was only 12 ft wide; the way to it from the north was from Starkholmes (301587). From Cromford Bridge eastwards the pre-turnpike route to Holloway makes a pleasant walk; it is shown on Burdett's map of 1767. The way follows the present road as far as the bend east of the railway bridge; the packhorse route then climbed past Woodend House before levelling out along the hillside, but this way is now private. However, a public footpath detours through the woods above the house and joins the old way in the fields below Meadow Woods Farm. It then joins the tarmac'd farm lane from Castletop, but leaves it again as a bridleway just below Bow Wood Farm; the old way, for long lengths roughly paved though grass-grown, continues through the woods, before descending to Lea Bridge. The way ahead climbs to Nether Holloway and then to Upper Holloway and must be so ancient that it had already become worn to a hollow by the beginning of the thirteenth century when 'Holeway' was first recorded; by the middle of the next century the name had become 'Holoweyes'. On many steep hillsides the original way became so deep and founderous that the packhorse trains were forced to start on a different zigzag up the hill then, after another cen-tury perhaps, on yet another new line. But where are these hollow-ways today? As Nether Holloway and Upper Holloway, the oldest parts of the sprawling village, are sited on the steepest section of the hillside, the ways between them presumably at one time gave them their names, but the area is now residential and old ways cannot be traced. The Enclosure Map of 1777 shows that a cross once stood at the top of the hill; it probably served as a sky-line landmark, confirming the former impor-tance of this route. The way forward to the north-east would approxi-mate to the line of the present footpath to Shuckstone Cross (342572), the stone base of which is still in position; two footpaths cross at this point and both must at one time have been important packhorse ways — that coming up from the site of Wakebridge Manor (338557) still serves as a parish boundary. From the site of the Upper Holloway Cross a footpath leads almost due north into a very good example of a worn way (332570-332575) towards Lea Hall; another footpath descends into this old way through a stile inscribed 'I.C.1789' and at this crossing the walker will be surprised to find a signpost.

The old way to Cromford Bridge from Wirksworth ran west of the present main road. Not far north of Wirksworth, beyond the fork for Middleton there is a minor fork (287546); this is Old Lane and can readily be followed through disused quarries and under the former Cromford and High Peak railway to emerge on Porter Lane (at 286555). A branch railway to quarries has interrupted the direct line of the old way, which would originally have formed a cross-roads with Porter Lane. The next section, Dark Lane, begins a short distance to the east and in rather less than half-a-mile joins the present road to Cromford. Slightly south of this junction another old way leads back through Bolehill (293550) and continues south-east through a hamlet called Packhorse.

From Wirksworth to the west the Romans constructed Hereward Street (p24) and this was probably used in much later times by pack-horses. At Carsington (251534), which lies close to the Roman road, a 'Jagger Waye' is referred to in a document of 1592; this was probably the road leading north from White House (234524) and forming the Car-sington-Brassington parish boundary. A half mile north of White House this road turns left, but a track goes straight forward and is followed by the parish boundary; the name 'Jaggerways' has persisted as the name of two fields near this boundary and, if the latter is taken as a guide, the jaggerway passed close to Harboro' Rocks (243554) to join the Chariot Way (p15).

SALT WAYS

For many centuries salt was a vital commodity for the preservation of meat. Part of a Roman soldier's pay was in the form of an allowance of salt (Latin *salis*); this was his *salarium*, whence our word 'salary'.

Salt occurs in the brine pits of Cheshire at Northwich, Middlewich and Nantwich. In Staffordshire there were less important brine pits at Baswich, near Stafford, and at Shirleywich, near Weston. In Worcestershire brine occurs at Droitwich. It will be noticed that all these place names end in 'wich'. In general this suffix is the Old English *wic*, a loan-word from the Latin *vicus* meaning a dwelling or group of dwellings. In the salt towns the suffix at first meant no more than the group of buildings around the brine pit, but the special meaning 'salt works' had already developed by the time that Domesday Book was being compiled.

Because salt was so necessary to daily life, it was transported from the salt pans over very long distances; carts drawn by oxen were used in the immediate neighbourhood, but for carriage further afield packhorses were employed. Each salter with his packhorse, or perhaps small train of packhorses, would follow a regular route from the 'wich' where he bought his salt, and these salters' routes became known as saltways. They were, of course, packhorse ways and no different from the ways used by other traders, but they can be followed from placenames, sup-ported in some instances by local tradition. The placenames embody the

119

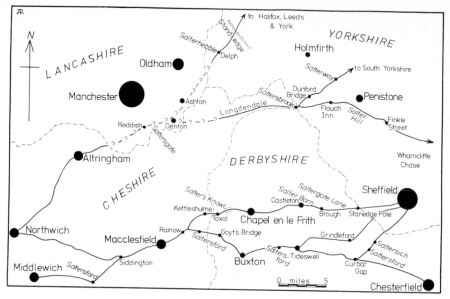

Map 41   Saltways in the northern part of the Peak District.

word 'salt', or more commonly 'salter': Saltersford, Saltersbridge, Salters Lane, Salters Well, Saltergate, etc. Several such names can be
traced back to Saxon charters, and Domesday Book names seven manors
in Cheshire holding salt rights from Saxon times. Tolls were levied on
the sale of salt, the rate being so much per cart-load, horse-load or man-
load. It is the routes along which the horse-loads were carried that interest us and we will describe some of those passing through the Peak
District, starting with the most northerly and working south. For much
of our information on these saltways we are indebted to the researches of
W. B. Crump.

A saltway left Northwich and passed through Altrincham and Reddish; from there the way was along Saltersgate to Denton making for the
crossing of the Pennines at Standedge (015100). The River Tame was
crossed near Delph (985079) by Salterhebble, 'hebble' being an old
northcountry word for a narrow bridge. There was another Salterhebble north of Elland on the way to Halifax, and a Saltergate and Salter
Lane on the route towards Leeds and York.

Further south, Cheshire had a long spur pushing between Lancashire
and Derbyshire to reach Yorkshire at Salters Brook (136002). The first
Earls of Chester claimed this way up Longdendale so that salt from their
county could be carried freely into Yorkshire. A route up Longdendale
was certainly an important saltway in medieval times, although there
are no placenames to determine the precise route from Northwich until
we reach Salters Brook itself; the original way from Woodhead was

north of, and above, the present road, which is crossed to arrive at the old bridge at Salters Brook, continuing south of the present road for about a mile to Lady's Cross. However, at Salters Brook the way divided. The more northerly route was via Dunford Bridge and Salterway, half way between Holmfirth and Penistone, and so into Yorkshire. The more southerly route passed the Flouch Inn (197016) and close to Hartcliff Tower to follow the ridgeway over Salter Hill (245010) to Finkle Street (303989); the saltway continued eastwards through High Green, Mortomley, Chapeltown, and then up to the ridge near Thorpe Hesley (where there is a Salter place name on an eighteenth century map) and so through Kimberworth to Rotherham.

A more southerly saltway leading to Sheffield left Cheshire via Macclesfield and Rainow; the way is roughly followed by the A5002 but beyond the fourth milestone out of Macclesfield, where the present road turns sharply east to Blackbrook Bridge, the old way continued north-north-east, crossing the A5002 at Charles Head on a direct course for Reed Bridge (983794). From Kettleshulme this old way was along Flatts Lane, up to Green Head and past Taxal church to a ford through the River Goyt. Near Horwich End the placename Salters Knowl (014807) confirms the route. The way forward would be over Eccles Pike (035-812), by Lidgate and the Crossings (047810) to Chapel en le Frith; in 1762 tolls on the turnpike here included 'Pack-horse carrying malt, salt, flour, corn or grain —½d; Pack-horse carrying other goods — 1 d'. The saltway continued over Peaslows to Sparrowpit and down the Winnats into Castleton. The Enclosure Map of 1819 for Hope Parish shows Salto Lane crossing the Hope to Pin Dale road and passing through the area now occupied by the cement works; Salto Lane would have passed Salter Barn at 168823. Two miles to the east Saltergate Lane climbs north-east from near Bamford Station, aiming for Sheffield via Stanedge Pole (247844). However, there is a Psalter Lane leading into Sheffield from Ecclesall, and in 1485 this was 'Salterlane'; evidently there was a still more southerly saltway to Sheffield than that just described, and as in the thirteenth century there was a Salterford at Tideswell we may assume that the route was via Great Hucklow and the Sir William Road to Grindleford, then by Fox House (266802) and Ringinglow (290837).

Tideswell also lay on a saltway from Cheshire to Chesterfield. Leaving Macclesfield as before on the Whaley Bridge road (A5002), the way branched off near Rainow to cross the Todd Brook at Saltersford (980767). It then climbed over Oldgate Nick (995763). From the west two hollow-ways aim for this notch in the skyline; that from Saltersford Farm, which bears the date 1593, follows the western spur of Cats Tor before curving up to the Nick; the other coming down 'The Corkscrew' to cross the Todd Brook at Burton, then climbs past Jenkin

54 Goyt's Bridge on a salt route through Buxton. When this area was flooded by Errwood Reservoir the bridge was rebuilt upstream.

Chapel (984765) named from a previously existing Jenkin Cross, probably a landmark. The way turns south-east between stone gateposts opposite Pym Chair Farm (991766). The east side of Oldgate Nick has been bulldozed, but beyond this recent disturbance a hollow-way descends towards the Street and would have crossed the old Goyt's Bridge (014751); since the Errwood Reservoir was constructed, the packhorse bridge has been re-erected about a mile upstream. From Goyt's Bridge the saltway continued through Buxton, where Salters Close is an old field name, out through Fairfield, across Great Rocks Dale to Hargatewall (117752) and so via the head of Monks Dale to cross Saltersford into Tideswell. The route eastwards to Chesterfield must have been over Calver Bridge and Curbar Gap (261747), but the only indication that this was a saltway is the name Saltergate, dating from 1285, leading into Chesterfield from Old Brampton. As there is a Salters Ford (282767) and a Saltersich (288780) near Owler Bar, there was presumably also a saltway linking Curbar to Sheffield. Also, a reference in 1659 to a Salterway at Chelmorton would indicate that some of the salters from Northwich may have left Macclesfield on the more southerly packhorse route (p94) through Flash and Washgate to Brierlow and Chelmorton.

In the neighbourhood of Brund (102612), where for centuries there has been a crossing of the River Manifold, tradition has lingered of another saltway leading to Chesterfield. At some of the farms there were mule stables with doorways wide enough to admit laden mules on their way from Nantwich to Chesterfield, where some of the salt was used for glazing coarse pottery. At that time the River Manifold at Brund was spanned by an ancient packhorse bridge, reputed to have defied Time and Water for so long because the mortar had been tempered with ale!

55 Brund Mill Bridge prior to 1891, when it was rebuilt. (J.P. Sheldon: *Through Staffordshire Stiles and Derbyshire Dales*, 1894)

But in 1891 it was deemed to be too narrow and was replaced by the present bridge. The way from Cheshire probably passed through, or close to, Leek and by Blakemere House (now the Mermaid Inn, 037605); keeping to the south side of Merryton Low, the way would follow the Warslow road for about a mile before bearing left over Lum Edge. Part of the line over Lum Edge is still a parish boundary although the ancient track on which it was based is now lost; so too, for the most part, is the way forward over Swallow Moss (from 065606 to 079611), but the whole line across this wet area of moorland was still shown on the 1840 OS map. On Reaps Moor the route of the old saltway is preserved as a metalled road to Field Head (088612); it then becomes a footpath (a lane between walls in 1840) leading directly into the short length of road to Brund Mill (100613). The route thus far is referred to in a lawsuit of 1749 as being 'used by packhorses who carry salt out of Cheshire into Derbyshire and Nottinghamshire', and it is stated that there was a stone causeway on the steep ascent of Morridge.

From the bridge near Brund Mill the saltway would follow the by-road along the northern flank of Sheen Hill and then down the green lane to ford the River Dove near Pilsbury (116635). From there the way climbed steeply from the valley, as does the present lane, but then probably made in a direct line over the hills past Custard Field (137640) to a point just north of the Benty Grange tumulus (146642); there the old way can be followed as a footpath which crosses The Street (p27) and then runs as a very broad green-way between walls as far as the Parsley Hay to Monyash road. If the line is then continued through old lead workings and across fields, it leads directly to a guidestone (156651), which now serves as a gatepost on the east side of Derby Lane (known locally also as Summerhill Lane). This guidestone is inscribed, one name on each face,

56 A saltway to Chesterfield came down this broad green way near Monyash.

Map 42 Saltways in the southern part of the Peak District.

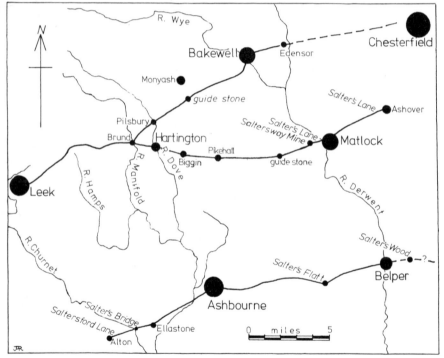

'Buxton, Chedel, Darby, Bakewell'. The saltway passes from the 'Chedel' (ie Cheadle, Staffs) side to the Bakewell side, turning down a field to enter the head of Fern Dale, down which a packhorse track can be traced to the top of Lathkill Dale near the old Ricklow Quarry. The way ahead would pass through Over Haddon to Bakewell and on to Chesterfield by one of the packhorse ways over East Moor (p103).

Some of the salters who crossed the Manifold at Brund Mill may have been on their way to Matlock Bridge, for there are 'Salter' place names in that area. A likely route, now merely a footpath, can be traced from the hamlet of Brund up the fields to Sheen and then over the hill to Hartington; local tradition maintains that this formed part of a long-distance packhorse route. From Hartington the way would have climbed past the Hall to Biggin as shown on a map of the Manor of Hartington dated 1614; this map does not mark any way up Hartington Dale. From Biggin a track (now a footpath) shown on Burdett's map of 1762-7 led to Pikehall; from there the salters would aim for what we have referred to as Guidestone 2 on Bonsall Moor (p116). If we now follow Bonsall Lane to Brightgate (265596) a footpath, evidently once an important way as it still marks a parish boundary, leads forward over land riddled with old lead mines, one of which was Saltersway Mine. For half a mile after the footpath has terminated the line of the saltway and the parish boundary follow a limestone outcrop and lead into Salters Lane, a name first recorded in 1621 and still in use. As it descends steeply to Matlock Bridge, Salters Lane turns sharp left; formerly the way was directly down the fields to the bridge. At Ashover, four miles north-east of Matlock Bridge there is another Salters Lane, so we may assume that salt was carried to Chesterfield via Matlock as well as via Bakewell.

A saltway into the southern part of the Peak District followed Saltersford Lane from the Tithebarn (074417) at Alton to a ford through the River Churnet. The ford must have been replaced by a bridge at an early date for it is recorded that by 1608 Salters Bridge (096418) was in need of repair; the bridge was still marked and named on the OS map of 1836 but has long since disappeared. From this crossing of the Churnet the way must have led through Ellastone to Ashbourne, where there is a Salt Alley. Perhaps this led to a place where salt was stored; in the *Derby Mercury* for the 27 April 1781, there appeared the following advertisement:

Messrs. Newton and Armstrong of Ashborne, Begs Leave to acquaint their Friends and the Public, that they have laid in a large Quantity of CHESHIRE SALT, which they are now selling at 19s 6d per Load, no less Quantity at the above Price. N.B. A Load of Salt is 16 Stone Nett.

One of the saltways from Ashbourne must have led through Belper; there is a fieldname Salters Flatt at Turnditch (295465) and a Salter Wood (388480) 2½ miles east of Belper. Perhaps this saltway led to Nottingham.

DROVERS' ROADS

Even in prehistoric times herds were driven from one grazing area to another and some of the 'British Trackways' marked on maps may have been ancient drovers' roads or drift-ways, as they were sometimes called; the names 'ox-road' or 'ox-way' are also occasionally met with.

Droving became important when cities had grown too big for all their meat to be supplied by the neighbouring countryside; the supply of meat to the Navy also became an important part of the drovers' trade. Cattle were being driven to London from Wales as far back as the fourteenth century. By the time of Elizabeth I drovers had become so numerous that it was deemed necessary to control them by Statute; it was enacted that every drover must be at least 30 years old and a married householder, and that his licence must be signed by three Justices of the Peace and be renewed each year. This law raised the status of the true drover; in addition to his prime task of driving cattle and sheep, he became a carrier of messages and, more important, a travelling banker. To prevent fraud, a law passed in the reign of Queen Anne forbade any drover from declaring himself bankrupt in order to escape from financial obligation. A drover often had £1,000 worth of beasts in his charge and it was soon realized that 'money on the hoof' was less vulnerable to robbers than was a saddle-bag filled with golden guineas; when a merchant in the provinces needed to pay a bill in some town or city on a drover's route he would pay the drover, who would leave the money at home and settle the bill from the proceeds of his sale at his journey's end. In South Wales, from where vast numbers of cattle were driven to London, drovers became the earliest bankers. In 1799 a Welsh drover named David Jones founded the Black Ox Bank at Llandovery, and notes engraved with a black ox continued to be issued until the First World War; this bank was eventually taken over by Lloyds.

The word 'drover' is apt to conjure up a picture of a hard-swearing hulk of a man belabouring his herd with a cudgel to hurry them on to the slaughter house. He probably was big and useful with his fists, and could doubtless swear with the best, but he knew that to get top price at Smithfield the animals in his charge must be in prime condition however far they had been driven. Beasts were not often driven more than a dozen miles in a day, with perhaps a rest day where there was suitable grazing; indeed, a law was passed in the reign of Charles I prohibiting the driving of cattle on Sundays, but this was for the good of the drover's soul rather than for the health of the beasts in his charge.

The size of driven herds varied greatly, but cattle were generally split up into herds of not more than two hundred with a drover to every fifty beasts; the drovers liked to see their herd moving at a gentle pace in a column two or three abreast. Sheep were driven in bigger herds, sometimes as many as two thousand. Dogs were used, then as now, and if their masters needed to spend a day or two in town attending to business, the dogs would often be sent back home by themselves: they would call at the same inns that their masters had used on the outward journey and the inn keepers would feed them. The rate of pay for a drover in the early nineteenth century was from two to three shillings a day — double the wage of a farm labourer; but the drover had to pay for his night's lodging, which might cost fourpence in the summer and sixpence in the winter. Even so, a drover could amass a modest fortune; one Welsh drover, who died in 1819, left £963 together with animals worth another £293.

Cattle were often driven several hundred miles and to protect their feet they were shod. Unlike the hoof of a horse, that of a bullock is cloven, so that eight small shoes were necessary for a complete shoeing; in the mid-nineteenth century the cost of this was a shilling per beast. Sheep were never shod. Geese were made to walk through a mixture of tar, sand and sawdust; the thought of a thousand geese on the march is rather daunting, but as many as 20,000 were driven to the famous Nottingham Goose Fair. Pigs wore woollen socks with leather soles to preserve their trotters; even so they progressed at no more than six miles a day. To prevent them from grubbing up the road or drift-way, they were often muzzled. The great days of droving coincided with the growth of cities during the Industrial Revolution; in the mid-eighteenth century, 100,000 cattle and 750,000 sheep were being driven to London annually. Droving declined with the coming of the railways.

The major drovers' roads converged on London from South Wales and, on the east, from Yorkshire and Scotland; a fine length of drovers' road on the east is Sewstern Lane, which runs parallel to the A1 west of Grantham. It is difficult to point to more than one long drovers' route in the Peak District. As far as possible, drovers kept to unenclosed moorland and commons; they avoided turnpike roads, where they would have had to pay tolls, until as they approached towns no alternative route was available. For evidence on the ground we can only look to the moorlands; elsewhere we must rely on placenames, drovers' inns, and tradition. Relevant placenames, in addition to 'ox' names, are Halfpenny Field or Penny Field, which may be fields once rentable overnight by drovers at ½d or 1d per beast; they are equally likely to be derisory names given to fields that are small.

A well-attested drovers' route through the Peak District from Cheshire to Nottingham is 'The Great Road from Congleton to Winster'. It climbs over Gun Hill, north of Leek, and then descends past Oxhay Farm to Meerbrook (990608). After crossing the Leek to Buxton road, the way led past Hurdlow Farm to Blakemere House (037605); this was at one time a drovers' inn, but has for many years had a mermaid as its sign. A mile north of the inn an area of moorland is known as Oxbatch. The drovers' route is said to have continued via Warslow to cross the River Dove at Hartington, and then on to Winster. Perhaps the way from

57   The Mermaid Inn, formerly Blakemere House, was at one time a drovers' inn on 'The Great Road from Congleton to Winster'.

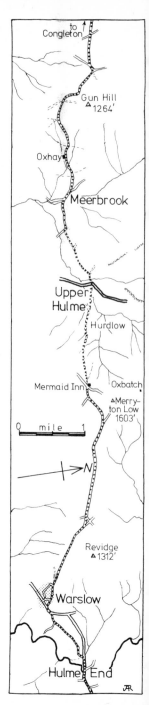

Map 43   Part of the drovers' road from Congleton to Winster.

Hartington was through Biggin (155594) and Newhaven (165593), where a cattle and sheep fair was held annually from at least as far back as the seventeenth century. If the way forward from Newhaven lay rather more to the south than through Winster, it could have tied in with a traditional drovers' road near Wirksworth, known as Summer Lane, leading from a point near Stainsboro' Hall (267532) to the Warmbrook suburb of Wirksworth. Summer Lane was recorded as Summer Way in 1420, presumably it was used only in the summer, becoming too founderous in the winter. From Warmbrook the way forward may have been up Gorsey Bank and over Alport Hill (305516). The Derwent would then be crossed at Ambergate; a mile to the north-east is Bullbridge, a name dating from the seventeenth century and suggesting a river crossing for cattle, and close by the bridge is a lane known as Drovers' Way.

Another drovers' route for which we have evidence is one from Scotland passing through Leek and Ashbourne. During Bonnie Prince Charlie's abortive rebellion in 1745, the Highlanders marched through Leek to Derby; three days later on the return march along the same road, one young Highlander dropped out with a broken ankle. He was hidden and cared for by a farmer at Apesford (017535); when immediate danger had passed the farmer waited for a band of drovers to go by on their way back to Scotland and persuaded them to take the Highlander home. As the road from Ashbourne through Leek to Macclesfield and the north, passing close to Apesford, had not then been turnpiked, the Scottish drovers may well have used this road rather than have kept to the Morridge moorlands.

Ashbourne may have been on more than one drovers' route, for Ashbourne Lane, leading in a southerly direction from Chapel en le Frith over Martinside to Dove Holes, is said to have been a drovers' road; it evidently provided a route from Cheshire to Ashbourne but, from Dove Holes, tradition has it that the drovers continued along the old way from Manchester to Derby described on p76. If this was indeed the route followed by drovers using Ashbourne Lane and making for Ashbourne, a driftway must have branched from the old Derby way, perhaps at Monyash. It may be relevant that not too far distant, there is another old north-south route part of which was formerly known as Ashbourne Lane: this is the way passing west of Tideswell, leading from Peak Forest through Wheston and thence directly into Miller's Dale, the last mile and a half being a green lane. This way, too, could well have led to Monyash, there joining the way that climbed the other Ashbourne Lane from Chapel en le Frith. The route followed by drovers and others from Monyash to Ashbourne, however, is by no means clear; it could have been via Pikehall and the way leading due south from there which was 'Le Heyweye' as far back as the thirteenth century.

6 The Turnpike Era

*This new Method of repairing the Highways at the
Expence of the Turn-pikes; that is to say, by the
Product of Funds rais'd at those Turn-pikes; it must
be acknowledg'd they are very great Things and very
great Things are done by them.*

Daniel Defoe, *A Tour thro' the whole Island
of Great Britain, 1724-6*

The first Act of Parliament permitting the levy of tolls to provide money
for the repair of a highway (part of the Great North Road) was passed in
1663, but it would seem that the road was not sufficiently improved for
the experiment to be soon repeated. There was greater success when a
later Act of Parliament (1706) created a Turnpike Trust and included
local landowners and other prominent local people as Trustees responsible for seeing that the intentions of the Act were carried out. During
the decade from 1720, over seventy Turnpike Acts passed through Parliament and it is therefore not surprising that the epigraph to this chapter
should continue 'and 'tis well worth recording, for the Honour of the
present Age, that this Work has been begun, and is in an extraordinary
Manner carry'd on, and perhaps may in a great Measure be compleated
within our Memory'.

The word 'turnpike' was used as early as 1477 in the Paston Letters,
where it refers to the gate to a walled town. The principle underlying
the turnpiking of a road was that Parliament authorized Trustees to set
up tollgates and collect tolls from travellers and others using the length
of road for which those Trustees were responsible. The tolls collected at
the gates generally had to be mortgaged in advance to provide the capital needed to begin improvements. It was at first thought that once a
road had been improved it would then be possible to keep it in repair by
the old Statute Labour method, and the early Turnpike Acts were therefore limited to 21 years at most, after which time Parliament intended
that the tollgates would be removed and travel would again be free.
Experience soon showed that proper maintenance could be as expensive
as road improvement, so that tolls had to be levied indefinitely.

In the early days of the Turnpike Era there were no road engineers and
the Trustees and their surveyors had to proceed by trial and error. Most
of the roads that they took over in the Peak District were packhorse

ways, which took little account of steep hills and in many cases, as we have seen, crossed unpopulated moors; many villages that were growing as a result of industry dependent on water power had to wait until the end of the eighteenth century before the Turnpike Trustees realized that it would be both more commodious and more profitable for coaches and waggons to follow populous valleys even where some old moorland route was more direct.

In addition to the numerous Acts of Parliament authorizing the setting up of individual Turnpike Trusts (by 1830 there were 3,783 such Trusts in England and Wales) there were a few general Acts relating to all turnpikes. One such general Act gave magistrates the power to sentence anyone found guilty of pulling down or damaging a tollgate to 'Transportation to one of His Majesty's Plantations Abroad for Seven Years'. Other general Turnpike Acts were concerned with the damage to the roads caused by heavy waggons with narrow wheels, and by the early nineteenth century there were also general regulations requiring that before work began on any new length of road, accurate plans should be prepared by a competent civil engineer. The General Highways Acts of 1766 and 1773 permitted those liable for Statute Labour on the roads to pay money in lieu; the 1835 Highways Act finally abolished Statute Labour and this was estimated by Macadam to have cost the Turnpike Trusts in England and Wales about £200,000. By this time railways were beginning to link the major cities and in 1837 the Turnpike Era had reached its zenith with a total revenue exceeding £1,500,000; in that year the London to Edinburgh mailcoach regularly completed its 373 mile run in 45½ hours, compared with the ten days in summer and twelve days in winter a century earlier. In the mid-1830s there were over 3,000

58   Toll receipt ticket at Cupola Bar, Ringinglow, 10 September 1850.

coaches on the roads of England requiring over 150,000 horses and 30,000 men — to maintain the elaborate coaching system that had by this time developed demanded not only coachmen, with a guard on each mail-coach, but also professional horse-keepers, farriers, and the many ostlers at posting inns. But by 1850 the days of the stagecoach were numbered; the total tolls collected at the Derbyshire gates fell from £38,145 in 1837 to £29,676 in 1854, and the tolls taken in Staffordshire fell in the same period from £57,102 to £43,459. After 1839 no more stage-coaches ran from London to Birmingham but in the Peak District, where railways came late, a mailcoach continued to run between Matlock and Manchester until October 1858 — one of the last mailcoaches in England. The *Weekly Telegraph* stage-coach was still operating between Sheffield, Bakewell and Buxton, three days a week and in summer only, even in 1895, but this must have been for 'nostalgia trade' much as steam trains are run today. By then all the tollgates had been thrown open, responsibility for highways having been transferred in 1888 to Local Government.

The organization of the Post Office mailcoaches owed much to John Palmer. The first route to benefit from his proposals was that from London to Bristol, and Palmer's first mailcoach, in August 1784, completed the 116 miles in 16 hours. On 26 July 1785, the Post Office advertised that 'Mr. Palmer's Plan for conveying His Majesty's Mails every day in the week (Sundays excepted) is extended to Liverpool, Manchester, Nottingham and Leeds'. The mailcoach route from London to Manchester was through Derby, Ashbourne, Leek and Macclesfield. Each mailcoach had its armed guard, who sat alone on the mailbox; the guard had charge of the coach and one of his duties was to blow a coaching horn at the approach to tollgates, which were promptly thrown open so as not to cause delay — mailcoaches were exempted from tolls by an Act of Parliament of 1785. The coaching horn was also sounded on approaching each posting inn, where horses were changed and passengers set down and taken up. The towns in the Peak District enjoying a daily post from London were, in 1814, Ashbourne, Bakewell, Buxton, Chapel en le Frith, Glossop, Matlock, Stoney Middleton, Tideswell and Wirksworth. The normal distance between posting inns was a dozen miles, perhaps less in hilly districts. The working life of the horses was three years for mailcoaches, four years for crack stage-coaches and up to seven years for the slower coaches; a four-horse coach had a team of five horses, one being at rest, and a team that did a morning stage would return over the same stage in the afternoon or evening. The coachman's average day was fifty miles.

Old prints and Christmas cards would make us believe that travel by stagecoach was quite a jolly affair; over a short distance on a pleasant

THE UNITED TRUST

of the

ASHFORD AND BUXTON, TIDESWELL AND BLACKWELL, AND EDENSOR AND ASHFORD
TURNPIKE ROADS.

£2 REWARD.

WHEREAS much injury has been done to the Walls on this Road, by mischievous or evil-disposed persons throwing down or otherwise damaging the same. Now therefore, NOTICE IS HEREBY GIVEN, that the above Reward will be paid by the Trustees of this Road, to any person or persons who shall give such Information and Evidence as shall lead to and result in the Conviction of any person so offending.

By Order of the Trustees,

ROBERT THORNHILL,

SURVEYOR.

59 Early nineteenth-century notice relating to wilful damage to walls alongside turnpike roads in the Peak District.

spring day so it doubtless was, but to take a coach from, say, Manchester through Buxton to Derby in the middle of winter could be hazardous. The following advice was given to outside passengers travelling in winter: 'They should drink a tankard of good ale cold from the tap, and rub their hands, ears and faces with snow immediately before they start'. It was not unknown for an outside passenger to freeze to death. But even setting aside the dangers of winter travel, there could be a general unpleasantness as is shown by a letter to a Sheffield newspaper in 1817:

Comfort is out of the question. Annoyances include the profanities of outside passengers, the smell of putrid game and fish, the long and chilly waits for connecting coaches, and the immense loads of luggage carried on the roof to the danger of passengers.

The number of passengers was limited by law to six inside, six outside, and two on the box, but in country districts this was often winked at; one country coach that met with an accident was found to have had thirty-four passengers 'in or about it'.

In the 1820s the cost of travel included 3d or 4d per mile for tolls levied on the coach. A man from Blackburn who in 1824 travelled via Manchester, Leek and Ashbourne to London recorded his expenses:

133

	£	s	d
From Blackburn to London outside	1	16	0
Tips to coachmen (5 at 1/-)		5	0
Guard		4	6
Refreshments at Manchester		1	6
Supper at Leek		2	6
Breakfast at Northampton		2	0
Spirits on the journey		2	0
	£2	13	6

Every tollhouse was supposed to display a list of tolls, but one writer complained that in Derbyshire this was often neglected. Tolls levied on the turnpike road from Matlock Bridge to Chesterfield were, in 1823:

	s	d
For every horse, mule or other beast drawing any coach &c		4
Any waggon &c using wheels of the breadth of 6in.		4
Ditto less breadth than 6in.		6
For every horse, mule or other beast laden or unladen and not drawing		1½
For every drove of oxen, cows or neat cattle (calves excepted) (per score)		10
For every drove of calves, hogs, sheep, lambs, per score		5
For every carriage with wheels of breadth 6in. or upwards loaded with any millstone or blocks of stone, or timber and drawn by 5 horses	2	6
For each horse exceeding that number	1	0
For every carriage with wheels of less breadth than 6in. and loaded as aforesaid	3	9
And for each horse exceeding 5	1	0

For pedestrians a wicket-gate was usually provided through which they could pass freely. Trustees sometimes made special concessions to their friends with carriages: thus in 1765 we find that Mrs Boothby, of Ashbourne, 'shall pay nothing at the Gate at Green Lane for going to take the benefit of the air but to pay upon journies further than Hanging Bridge'.

For the toll collector a small house, often costing less than £50 to build, was erected by the gate, generally as close to the edge of the road as possible; eventually, after tolls ceased to be taken, toll-houses were usually sold and may still stand inhabited, even if much altered. Originally, toll-collectors were appointed by the Turnpike Trustees at a fixed wage, in the mid-eighteenth century perhaps five shillings a week but rent free; we have seen an agreement, dated 1766, for one toll-collector's wage to be at the rate of two shillings for every pound collected, but such an agreement was unusual. It was soon found more convenient and profitable to the Trustees to auction the gates, bids being made on the basis of the previous year's takings; in this way a new profession, toll-contracting, developed, one man often taking several tollgates along a particular turnpike. It is amusing to learn that in 1807

De Quincey, travelling through the night, found that each tollgate was opened for him (after due payment) by means of a mechanical contrivance from the bedroom window.

Coachmen, carriers and drovers were generally well acquainted with the roads they used, but not so the ordinary traveller. As we have seen (p 83) even in pre-turnpike days Parliament had ordered that guidestones or guideposts be erected at important crossroads; in 1798 the Derbyshire Justices ordered that signposts be erected at all necessary places in the county. Turnpike Acts passed in 1766 and in 1773 directed that milestones be set up on turnpikes; their design varied from Trust to Trust and a change in pattern along a road will indicate the boundary between one turnpike and another. It is no new thing for signposts and milestones to be targets for vandals: in his book on Derbyshire published in 1817, John Farey castigated

Map 44   The principal turnpike roads in the Peak District.

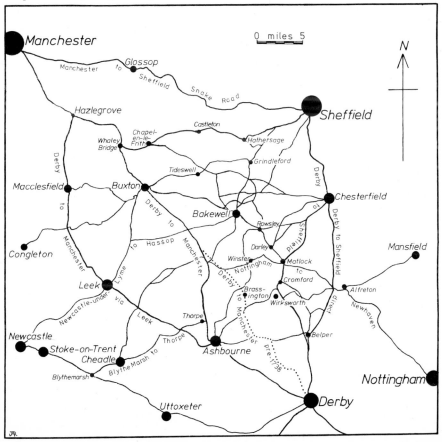

those idle and disorderly persons who now so shamefully deface the Milestones by their wanton and mischievous attacks on them, and on...the Way-posts or Finger-boards...scarcely a single inscription remains legible, from the peltings of the idle vagabonds above alluded to.

In the eighteenth century the three major roads passing through the Midlands were the Great North Road from London through York to Edinburgh, the road from London through Derby and Manchester to Carlisle, and the road from London to Chester for the passage to Ireland; early in the following century the Irish mail was transferred to the route via Shrewsbury and Holyhead. Of these three major roads, only that from London to Manchester passed through the Peak District; parts of this road were the first in our area to be turnpiked and so, both chronologically and in order of importance, this must be the first turnpike to be considered. It traversed the western side of the Peak District; the eastern side was served by the Birmingham-Derby-Chesterfield-Sheffield road. The cross-link on the north was from Sheffield to Manchester. Amongst the hills and dales bounded by these three major outer links, a complex network of cross-country turnpikes developed as will be seen on Map 44.

6.1 The Derby to Manchester Turnpike

As we have already seen (p76) the Derby to Manchester road of 1675 for most of its length followed the Roman road; this same line was being used half a century later, as shown on Herman Moll's map of Derbyshire published in 1724. In the south, the first section to be turnpiked, in 1738, was from the former ferry at Shardlow, south-east of Derby, to Brassington (232544), which is a rather obscure village at which to terminate a major turnpike. To find a reason for this we must remember that during the earlier part of the eighteenth century Parliament looked on turnpiking as a temporary measure to get a road made good; the London to Manchester road needed such attention over Defoe's 'clayey, dirty part' of the Midlands and the Act of 1738 was 'to amend the dangerous, narrow and at times impassable road'. But once on the well-drained limestone, the old Roman road was still adequate for the traffic of the day, and the road leading into Buxton from the south became known as London Road, the name that it still bears. North of Buxton, beyond the limestone, road improvement was again necessary and was authorized by Parliament in 1724, when the road through Whaley Bridge to Manchester was turnpiked. An amending Act of 1731 allowed increased tolls: 'Whereas the manner of carriage over the said roads was usually by packhorses, and by the great amendment and widening of the said roads is of late changed into wheeled carriage, whereby the said tolls have been greatly diminished'; this was because one six-horse waggon could carry as much as thirty packhorses. However, although in 1727 Defoe had found 'smooth green riding' along the Brassington to Buxton length of this major highway, the Earl of Egmont travelling north by private coach in 1744 recorded 'all the road entirely bad' and took over five hours to cover the sixteen miles from Derby to Brassington, where he was forced to stay the night. In their first six years the new turnpike surveyors had made little impression on the general state of their road.

One of the earliest users of these turnpikes was James Pickford, the eighteenth-century Cheshire carrier whose family name is still perhaps the best known in the transport business. An advertisement was inserted in the *Manchester Mercury*, 17 August 1756, by James Pickford 'the London and Manchester waggoner'; his waggons at that time covered about twenty miles in a day. In 1776 Pickfords introduced 'fly-waggons' which, light and well sprung, did the Manchester-Buxton-Derby-London journey in 4½ days, averaging 42 miles a day. By 1803 this service was running six days a week, travelling on alternate days via Buxton or via Macclesfield and Leek, and ten years later waggons leaving Manchester at 6pm were arriving in London on the next morning but one. As a side-line Pickfords also entered the mail-carrying business, but on 5 April 1795 the Post Office threatened to terminate their contract for carrying mail between Manchester and Macclesfield because 'Mr. Pickford... has lost much time and having other great occupations does not attend to the Coach duty'. The threat must have had its effect for two years later Pickfords were still carrying mail along this route.

60   Artist's impression of an eighteenth-century waggon.

Some of Pickfords waggons carried passengers, but special 'flying machines' for passengers, introduced by John Hanforth and partners in March 1760, covered the Manchester-Buxton-Derby-London journey in three days. In April 1765, the 'flying machines' were replaced by 'Post

Coaches calculated for Pleasure and Safety on the Genteelest Construction and most elegant Taste'. These coaches completed the Manchester to London run in two days with an overnight at Leicester; the fare from Manchester was 50 shillings and from Derby 28 shillings.

As we have seen, the Derby to Brassington and Manchester to Buxton roads were turnpiked at a very early date and it was soon realized that the original routes, with their formidable hills, left much to be desired; even the section south of Brassington, all below 1,000 feet, was described as 'monstrous hilly'. The 1738 Act had also authorized the turnpiking of an improved route from Derby through Ashbourne to Hurdlow (128-666); then in 1749 the Manchester-Buxton turnpike was extended southwards to link at the same point. The Brassington turnpike was still being mentioned in the *Derby Mercury* in 1780, but Farey states that the steep hills around Hognaston (235505) and other defects had caused virtual abandonment of the Derby-Brassington-Hurdlow route by 1817 except by local inhabitants: 'Travellers in general go by Ashburne... although such is considerably further about'. The Hulland Ward to Brassington end of this early turnpike was officially 'disturnpiked' in 1827 on the ground that 'this road led to no City, Town or Place of importance'. The original Loughborough Trust turnpike into Derbyshire thus became the 'Cavendish Bridge to Hulland Ward road'; Cavendish bridge had in 1761 replaced the old Trent ferry.

The Ashbourne to Buxton road as turnpiked in 1738 did not follow its present line (A515) through Fenny Bentley. In Ashbourne market square there is a fine cast-iron milestone of the late Turnpike Era, but there is a very early turnpike milestone, 'From London CXL', on the roadside near the Ashbourne end of the Tissington Trail, and a similar but indecipherable milestone a mile further towards Mapleton (166481). These two milestones are grey and slate-like; the source of the stone used has been identified by Martyn Owen, of the Institute of Geological Sciences, as Swithland (Charnwood Forest). It is of some interest that in the mid-eighteenth century, when the transport of heavy goods was still difficult, a Turnpike Trust was prepared to bring these milestones from a quarry many miles away when good sandstone was available within five miles.

These early milestones are strong evidence that Mapleton lay on the 1738 turnpike, which is likely to have been based on a packhorse way linking villages. More evidence is provided by an advertisement which appeared in the *Derby Mercury* in 1753 referring to the sale of Broadlowash (159502) 'upon the turnpike road from Ashburne to Buxton'. This suggests that the early turnpike continued from Mapleton to Spendlane Farm and then passed close to Broadlowash. However, Burdett's map of 1762-7 shows the turnpike running via Sandybrook (178482) and Red

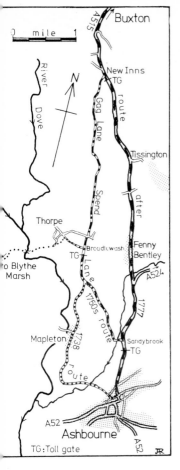

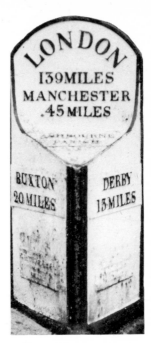

61 (*above left*) Milestone on the 1738 Ashbourne-Buxton turnpike.

62 (*above right*) Later cast-iron milepost (made by J. Hayward of Derby) on the 1777 route of the Ashbourne-Buxton turnpike.

Map 45   Part of the Ashbourne-Buxton turnpike.

House (173487) before linking with the original line along Spend Lane and Gag Lane to the New Inns (157546). Then in 1777 the Trustees made four miles of new road from Sandybrook past Tissington Gates to join the original road just short of New Inns; this is shown as 'New Inn' on Burdett's map but was already being referred to as 'New Inns' in the *Derby Mercury* in 1781. There was a rough road along here when Burdett prepared his map in 1762-7, and another country road linked Tissington via the ford through Bradbourne Brook to Bradbourne; on the south of this road down to the ford there is an old milestone (189521). Another, perhaps older, milestone stands on private ground in Tissington village.

On the original turnpike there was a tollgate a short distance to the north of New Inns, but when the new road was made in 1777 this toll-gate was moved to the junction of the old and new roads south of New Inns; the tollhouse was demolished in about 1965. The route forward to

Hurdlow was the line of A515 via the important road junction at New-haven. Until 1795 the only hostelry along the twenty miles between Ashbourne and Buxton was 'a mean public house nearly opposite the nine mile stone' which stands at Newhaven; there is still an old milestone there (165601) now mostly illegible. The Duke of Devonshire then rendered travellers a service by building, at this turnpike junction, 'a large handsome and commodious inn, where travellers meet with every requisite accommodation'. There is a tradition that one such traveller was George IV, who was so pleased with his entertainment that he granted the inn a free and perpetual licence. It was at first called the Devonshire Arms; perhaps the name was changed when the inn became part of the Duke of Rutland's estate at some time in the last century. Bank House Farm, a mile south of Newhaven, also seems to have been rebuilt to serve as a coaching inn early in the nineteenth century. On the 1840 OS map it is named 'Dean of Arlington's Arms' — perhaps there was no signboard when the surveyor came this way so that he had to ask the name and then mis-heard the reply, for it was the Dean of Hartington's Arms; the Deanery was abolished in 1858. To add to the confusion the coat of arms over the porch, dated 1856, is that of T.O. Bateman of Middleton by Youlgreave, who had bought this coaching inn. Yet another old inn is the Bull i' th' Thorn, some five miles north of Newhaven; it was originally Hurdlow House and was near a former crossroads named in 1654 as 'Hordlow Thorn otherwise Hordlow Cross'.

From the Bull i' th' Thorn the original un-turnpiked road followed the Roman road (p29) to Brierlow but at some date after 1749 the present road was constructed, veering west near Street Farm on a steadier gradient to Brierlow. There were also considerable changes over the years in the turnpike as it entered and left Buxton. The original (1724) turnpike from Manchester came into Buxton over a bridge spanning the Wye, passed east of the Old Hall, veered somewhat to the west and ascended Hall Bank into Upper Buxton. The Manchester turnpike terminated at Sherbrook Hill, now in Buxton's suburbs, and the way south continued through Harpurhill to Brierlow Bar, where there is an old milestone (From London 157) at the southern end of the forecourt of the petrol station; it was discovered when the tollhouse was demolished in the early 1920s — face down in use as a door-step. In 1781 the road through 'the hamlet of Buxton' was diverted from the new bridge near the Grove Coffee House (now the Grove Hotel) to the south-east corner of the old bridge, and from the north end of this old bridge (which was near the George Hotel) 'to the north-west corner of the Dissenting Meeting House'. A dozen years later the Crescent was built, its western end obliterated the old road and the Wye was culverted.

In 1762 a better route from Derby to Manchester became available

63 The Newhaven Hotel built in 1795 with stabling for 100 horses.

64 Bank House Farm was once a coaching inn — the Dean of Hartington's Arms.

with the turnpiking of the road between Ashbourne and Leek; this linked with the road from Leek through Macclesfield to Hazelgrove, where the latter joined the Buxton to Manchester turnpike. For the first mile out of Ashbourne towards Hanging Bridge, the road is straight and level; it was cut in 1763, being one of the first improvements that the newly created Trust carried out. However, once over Hanging Bridge the turnpike still followed the steep lane ahead (Old Bank) into Upper Mayfield, until the present easier route bypassing that village was made in 1786. Yet the new road up Swinscoe Hill was, and still is, both long and steep. The crack *Telegraph* coach, which regularly did the 187 mile run from Manchester through Leek and Ashbourne to London in 18 hours 17 minutes inclusive of breaks for two meals, came to grief on this hill on New Year's Day 1830, as is related in the *Staffordshire Advertiser*:

The coachman was accidentally thrown off his box and pulled a passenger down with him. The horses experiencing liberty, went down the hill at full speed, crossed the bridge at the bottom, and carried the coach with great violence against the corner of the public-house on the opposite side, forcing off one of the wheels. They then galloped towards the toll-bar, where the coach came in contact with the gate-post and was dashed almost to pieces ... The guard and coachman, it is feared, were far from being sober, as they had called at many inns on the road to drink, in commemoration of the day.

The tollgate hit by this coach was at the junction with Green Lane, which leads to Clifton. A little way up Swinscoe Hill there was a side-gate across Birdsgrove Lane, and the tollhouse still stands with a recess above the central window for the table of tolls.

Five miles out of Ashbourne, at Calton Moor, the Leek turnpike was crossed by the Blythe Marsh to Thorpe turnpike (p178) and in a further half mile we reach the landmark known as Miles Knoll, where the original route was straight ahead down what is now a narrow lane; the turnpike was altered to its present line in 1824. At the request of the Post Office, a plan for further improvement was drawn up by Telford, but the estimated cost (£16,000) was far too great for the Turnpike Trust to undertake.

The River Hamps is crossed at Waterhouses and again at Winkhill; immediately beyond Winkhill Bridge a track climbs to a farm and continues to rejoin the main road at Newstreet (055519) — this farm track was the original turnpike; the present road was cut in 1831. Just north of Newstreet the Ellastone turnpike comes in on the west, and the Cheadle-Butterton Moor turnpike (p177) crosses at Bottom House. Beyond Cook's Hollow and rather less than two miles short of Leek is Pool Hall Tollhouse, built in 1828 when the embankment was thrown up across the valley below and a new length of road cut on the hillside to

65 Tollhouse near Sutton, Macclesfield, on the Leek to Manchester road.

come into Leek under Lowe Hill Bridge. The original road can still be
followed, first as a footpath which passes in front of the old Lowe Hill
Tollhouse (997557) and then as a byroad which joins the present road
near the first milepost out of Leek. The iron mileposts on this turnpike
are of unusual design; they were cast by James Bassett of Ashbourne in
1834.

North of Leek the road to Manchester as far as Hazelgrove was the
responsibility of the Sandon to Bullock Smithy Turnpike Trust, authorized in 1761; Bullock Smithy, named from Richard Bullock who in 1560
leased land there on which to build a smithy, stood near the junction of
this turnpike with that from Buxton through Whaley Bridge and Disley.
John Byng rode along the turnpike from Manchester to Leek in June 1792
(a later journey than when he used the Buxton to Ashbourne turnpike);
between Macclesfield and Bosley Marsh he found the road 'exceedingly
pleasant, of a reddish sandstone'. A mile south of Macclesfield a tollhouse still stands at the end of Robin Lane, leading to Sutton.

John Byng had turned aside at Bullock Smithy to spend the night at
the Ram's Head, Disley, which in 1792 was evidently well-known. This
inn stood on the important Manchester to Buxton road, turnpiked in
1724 when it still followed the Roman route, climbing from Buxton past
White Hall and down Elnor Lane to Whaley Bridge, then over Longside
to Disley with yet another climb over Jackson's Edge to High Lane
('Hoo Lane' in the early nineteenth century). According to Dr George
Bew, writing in 1782, John Metcalf — the famous Blind Jack of Knares-

66   John Metcalf — Blind Jack of
Knaresborough — who surveyed and
supervised the construction of several
roads in the Peak District.

67 Blind Jack's original Old Longhill Road north of Buxton (foreground) with the later, gently graded, road in the background.

borough — was responsible for the improvement of many of the roads in the Peak District and particularly those in the vicinity of Buxton. It is probable that he set out the route of the present road from Buxton to Whaley Bridge (A5002) and on to Disley (A6). Yet scope for minor improvements remained. For example, Blind Jack reduced the climb up Long Hill, north of Buxton, from the summit of the Roman road at 1,500 ft to a summit of 1,394 ft; but his instinct and experience would then seem to have failed him, for having attained this lower summit (032752) by a steady and not too severe gradient, he plunged down what is now Old Longhill Road into a side valley of the River Goyt, losing 250 ft in height and having to climb some 60 ft to regain the general level of his road. The present long loop round the head of this side valley appears to have been constructed around 1820, Blind Jack's 1 in 6 hill being avoided at the cost of an extra three-quarters of a mile, a distance that coach-horses could more than make up by being able to trot on the new 1 in 35 gradient.

It was by such improvements that the mailcoaches were able to reduce their Manchester to London schedules from 60 hours in 1760 to 18¼ hours in 1830. The Manchester to Buxton Turnpike Trustees were granted their final Act of Parliament in 1860, when they owed £45,693 to the mortgagees, secured on their various roads. The Act directed that the Trustees should pay 3½ per cent interest, that not more than £2,500 be spent on the roads during the next year and not more than £2,000 in subsequent years, and that any profits be used to repay the mortgagees, those being paid first who were willing to compound at the lowest figure. Under these terms the Trust struggled on for another thirteen years, but was finally wound up on 1 November 1873. One of the assets

144

disposed of in that year was a toll-house on Alsop Moor 'on the west side of the Turnpike with two gardens belonging'.

6.2 Birmingham-Derby-Chesterfield-Sheffield

The turnpike left Birmingham in a northerly direction to Lichfield but then turned north-east along Ryknield Street (p 23) through Burton to Derby. By 1764 a stagecoach service between Birmingham and Sheffield was being advertised in the *Derby Mercury*; passengers slept at Derby and on the northward journey they then breakfasted at Matlock, dined at Chesterfield and reached Sheffield the same night. From Derby the coach would have been travelling on a road turnpiked in 1756 when a Trust was set up to improve the roads linking Derby, Chesterfield and Sheffield; also the branch road from Duffield to Wirksworth. The Wirksworth route from Duffield would at that date be via Hazelwood and over the Chevin to Crossroads Farm (336478), beyond which is Sandyford where there is a finely made milestone; rather more than a mile further on is the Bear Inn, at that time a coaching inn. The original turnpike continued over Wirksworth Moor to Cromford, round the Scarthin Rock (not yet blasted through) and so into Matlock. The road from there to Chesterfield set out up the appropriately named Steep Turnpike; this road was turnpiked in 1760 and was based on Hereward Street (p 24). In 1771 there were tollgates at Amber Lane near Slack (333628) and in Slatepit Dale (347680). In 1817 there were tollgates on the three turnpikes from Chesterfield leading respectively to Matlock Bridge, Darley Bridge and Rowsley Bridge at the following points: Walton Lane, Slatepit Dale, Hall Moor, Amber Lane, Hascar Lane, Buntingfield, Darley Bridge, Little Rowsley and Toadhole. However, in addition to these routes to Chesterfield, the 1756 Act had authorized the more direct turnpike road from Derby through Holbrook to Pentrichlane End (376518) and Oakerthorpe, and from there north along Ryknield Street.

Such was the limited road system around Matlock in early turnpike days. Certainly this was better than in 1724 when Defoe said that Matlock Bath had 'a base, stony, mountainous Road to it, and no good Accommodation when you are there'. As so frequently happens, it was industry that brought good communications to the area. Sir Richard Arkwright established his first cotton mill at Cromford in 1771 and it was he who made what was for many years a private road along the valley. Turnpiking came with an Act of Parliament passed in 1817 'For making and maintaining a Turnpike Road from the Town of Cromford to the Town of Belper and for making a Branch of Road from and out of said Road near the River Amber to join the Turnpike Road at Bull

68 (*above*) The Bear
Inn, a coaching inn on
Wirksworth Moor.

69 (*right*) Milestone
at Sandyford on the
original Derby to
Matlock turnpike.

70 (*below*) The Grey-
hound Hotel,
Cromford, built by
Sir Richard Arkwright
as a coaching inn.

Map 46   Part of the
Derby-Chesterfield
turnpike.

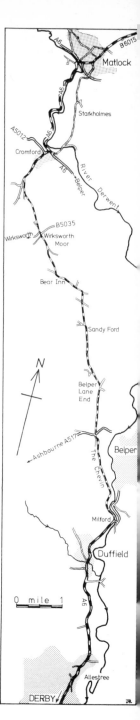

71, 72   The aptly named Steep Turnpike at Matlock, coming into the town from Chesterfield.

Bridge'. A tollgate was set up at the intersection with this branch road, and the hamlet that developed near this gate soon became known as Ambergate. According to Glover this new turnpike was opened in 1820 and was 'undoubtedly the best road for carriages of every description; and we need not scruple to say it will ultimately become the direct mailroad between Manchester and London'. But when Glover wrote these words in 1829 the Railway Age had already begun.

73   The three tollgates at Ambergate, about 1875; the railway is on the right.

74 The Winnats, Castleton, in Victorian times, with
its 1 in 5 gradient. Once on a saltway from Cheshire to
Sheffield, it became part of the 1758 Sheffield-
Manchester turnpike until bypassed in 1811 by the Mam
Tor route.

75 Hunter's Bar, Sheffield, still preserves the original
tollbar gateposts.

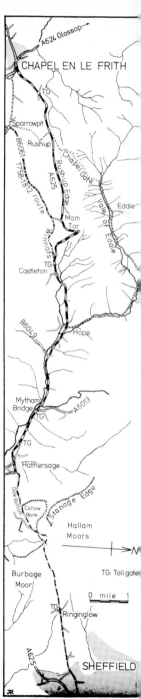

Map 47 Part of the Manchester-Sheffield turnpike via
Castleton.

6.3 Sheffield to Manchester

Burdett's map of 1762-7 depicts inaccessible moorland west of Sheffield; the Woodhead road is marked to the north and the Hathersage to Castleton road to the south, but two centuries ago the high ground between must have been wild indeed. The earliest coachroad developed from the various packhorse ways linking villages, the first part to have been turnpiked being in the west, from Manchester to Chapel en le Frith in 1724; in 1749 this was extended eastwards through Sparrowpit to Peak Forest, but the linking turnpike from Sparrowpit to Sheffield was not promoted and authorized until 1758. The route from Sheffield, before improvement, was via Ringinglow to Upper Burbage Bridge (261830) and down the very steep Callow Bank (now only a footpath) into Dale Bottom and Hathersage, where an early turnpike milestone — Sheffield 10 miles — is preserved on the north side of the main street. From Hathersage the turnpike continued through Hope to cross the Derwent at Mytham Bridge (205826) where there was a smithy and where a toll-house was erected; the old bridge of four arches was washed away in the flood of 7 August 1856. From Castleton the 1758 turnpike followed the packhorse route up the Winnats with its 1 in 5 gradient. At that period the Winnats must have been a lonely place and, in the very year when the road was turnpiked, a young couple on their way to be married clandestinely at Peak Forest were robbed and murdered in the pass and their bodies thrown into the Speedwell Mine. Forty years later, when Samuel Coleridge found himself in Sheffield, although to travel along this road may have become safer, it could still be tedious: 'Tomorrow morning I set off for Manchester at six o'clock — it is only 48 miles distant — and the coach will not arrive till ten o'clock at night. By heavens! a tortoise would outgallop us.'

Coleridge's slow-travelling coach would not have had to negotiate the steep hills at Peaslows (085808) and Eccles Pike (035812) as this switchback route from Sparrowpit westwards had been superseded in 1764 by detours via Barmoor Clough (now A623) and Tunstead Milton (now A6). Neither, earlier on his journey from Sheffield, would he have descended the precipitous Callow Bank into Hathersage; this formidable hill had been by-passed prior to 1767 by the making of a new loop north via Overstones Farm. However, this Dale Bottom way into Hathersage was still unsatisfactory and in 1811 it was abandoned and a new road was made from Fiddler's Elbow (259827) over Booth's Edge to enter Hathersage from the south-east. The same year (1811) saw the cutting of a new road from Castleton up the unstable flank of Mam Tor — 'Shivering Mountain' — continuing below the line of Rushup Edge direct to Chapel en le Frith.

During the early part of the nineteenth century, Pickfords operated a waggon service along this turnpike. The first stage out of Sheffield was Castleton — 16 miles in 8 hours — where two horsekeepers and a lad were maintained for 35s per week, and the annual rent of the stable (straw provided) was £18 12s 0d. The next stage was Bullock Smithy (Hazelgrove), a further 16 miles, where two horsekeepers were employed at 32s per week and the stable rent was £11. The last stage was the easy 9 miles into Manchester and only two waggoners were employed on this section compared with four on each of the hilly stages; all the waggoners received 25s per week which was then very good pay. Tolls were taken at Hunter's Bar, Booth's Bar, Whaley Bridge, Stockport Moor, Heaton Norris, Rushton and Longsight; with four horses, this meant that each waggon paid £2 12s 6d in tolls as it trundled between Sheffield and Manchester, and in the course of a year Pickfords paid £1,123 in tolls for their two waggons operating on this route.

A glance at the map will show that the Castleton route from Sheffield to Manchester was indirect; as traffic between these rapidly growing towns increased, speedier communications became imperative and in 1818 Parliament sanctioned a new road over the Snake Pass (A57). The greatest road engineer of the day, Thomas Telford, was engaged and this was one of his last projects. Telford's road leaves Sheffield along the Rivelin Valley and comes down to the River Derwent via Cutthroat Bridge, which acquired its gruesome name in the seventeenth century; a deposition dated 1635 reads: 'Found a man with a wound in his throat in Eashaw Clough...carried him to the house at Lady Bower'. The road passed through the hamlet of Ashopton, formerly known as Cocksbridge, which stood at the confluence of the Derwent and the Ashop and now lies submerged by the Ladybower Reservoir; in 1824 a road from Derwent village (185885) to Ashopton was made by the Newdigate family of Derwent Hall. From Ashopton there was already a bridleroad up the Woodlands Valley and Telford used this as a basis for his road on that side, but on the Glossop side of the pass he constructed an entirely new road — Snake Road — which attains a height of 1,680 ft and is one of the highest turnpikes in England. In 1821, shortly after the new road had been opened, an inn was built towards the top of the Woodlands Valley; it was at first known as Lady Clough House, from the clough above which it stands, but this name was soon changed to Snake Inn as a tribute to the Duke of Devonshire whose crest was a snake. Along this new turnpike milestones were erected giving the distances to 'Manc' and 'Sheff'. Tolls were collected at Moscar, Ashopton, Broom Spring, Snake Inn, Cross Poll and Woodcock Road; the last named tollhouse still exists (055943). In 1845, when traffic was already dwindling because of the railways, the total tolls collected at the six gates amounted to little

150

76 (*above*) A MANC/ SHEFF milestone on the Snake Road.

77 (*top right*) The Snake Inn, originally Lady Clough House.

78 (*right*) Woodcock Road tollhouse east of Glossop.

more than £10 a week, and in 1849 the Trustees were in debt to the tune of £107,000, much of this vast sum being floating debts due to the Duke of Devonshire and the Duke of Norfolk. Here is an illuminating example of an excellently engineered and potentially useful turnpike made too late for it to be profitable.

6.4 Cross Country Turnpikes from the East

Derby and Sheffield acquired direct communication with Manchester and Birmingham very early in the Turnpike Era. Nottingham soon sought a link with the road from London to Manchester and the north-west, and the Nottingham to Newhaven Turnpike Trust was created by Act of Parliament in 1759; Newhaven (166601), as we have already noted, is on the Derby to Manchester turnpike, and with the construction of additional cross country turnpikes the coaching inn there became important and well esteemed. The Act of 1759 was comprehensive and the new Trust was responsible for the roads in four Districts:

1st District — Nottingham to Newhaven
2nd District — Oakerthorpe to Ashbourne
3rd District — Wirksworth Moor to Longstone
4th District — Selston to Annesley Woodhouse

The Nottingham to Newhaven turnpike, the principal road administered by the Trust bearing its name, was always referred to in the Trust's Minute Books as the Alfreton Turnpike Road. It had the generous width of 60 ft and began in Nottingham at Hyson Green, proceeding to Alfreton via Selston, where the short Fourth District turnpike provided a link with the Mansfield road. The George at Alfreton was a coaching inn, the first stage out of Nottingham. With fresh horses, coaches would continue to Fourlane Ends, where the Belper to Chesterfield turnpike was followed to Oakerthorpe; there the Peacock Inn, dating from 1613, provided changes of horses for as many as sixteen coaches a day. From the fork to Wessington travellers would once more be on the Nottingham to Newhaven turnpike, now A615, arriving in nine miles at Matlock Bridge. At the first meeting of the Trust, 2 May 1759, it was ordered that a tollgate be erected in Smithy Lane on the west side of Matlock Bridge; five years later the Trustees directed that this gate be removed and re-erected across Causeway Lane. Several turnpikes met at Matlock, each with its own tollgate: Warm Wells Gate at Matlock Bath; Holt Lane Gate in Matlock Dale near Artists' Corner; Matlock Bank; Darley Dale; and Tansley Gate. The Matlock Bank tollhouse still stands at the bottom of Steep Turnpike. It was complained that 'in five directions Toll-bars are placed very near to this Town, one hilly and indifferent Lane only remaining open, towards Willersley, by which the Inhabitants can stir abroad without paying Tolls'; this did not apply to pedestrians, who could pass freely.

The pattern of the early turnpikes around Matlock is complex but seems to have been as shown on Map 48. A notable feature of this map is the absence of any road along the valley bottom, now traversed by the A6. Prior to the damming of the River Derwent in its upper reaches, first by the Derwent Reservoir and subsequently by the additional Ladybower Reservoir, the valley was frequently flooded. Defoe rightly called the Derwent 'a fury of a river... a frightful creature when the hills load her current with water'. For this reason the old villages of Snitterton, Hackney and Northwood were wisely sited well up the valley sides. So the Newhaven turnpike, having crossed Matlock Bridge, climbed to

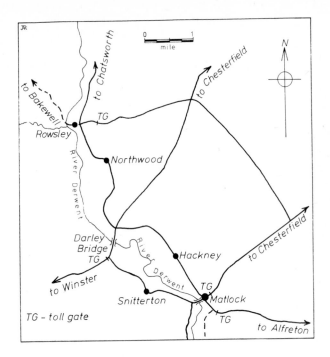

Map 48   The turnpike system near Matlock in 1760 (diagrammatic).

the village of Snitterton, where one of the original milestones — London 159, Nottm. 26 — confirms that we are still on the Nottingham turnpike. It continued up the western flank of Oaker Hill (272614), one of the hills referred to by the Trustees at a meeting on 17 August 1767: 'It is impracticable for any Wagon or other 4 wheeled Carriage with the weights allowed by the Act of Parliament without manifest inconvenience and hazard to be drawn up'. They allowed extra horses (ten horses for waggons with broad wheels) and the Trust's surveyor was directed to set up stones or posts to mark the point at the bottom of the hill where the extra horses could be hitched and the point at the top where they must be unhitched. Beyond Oaker Hill the Newhaven turnpike was joined by the 'Toadhole Turnpike' from Chesterfield; bearing west it climbed another hill on which extra horses were allowed and so came into Wensley (263611). At their first meeting in 1759 the Trustees had ordered that a gate and tollhouse should be erected at Wensley, but ten months later they realized (or had been told by the gate-keeper!) that this tollhouse had been inadequately designed: 'Ordered that an addition of an oven to bake bread and a Necessary House with 2 seats be made'. This euphemism for a privy derives from the *Necessarium* of the monasteries and, abbreviated to 'Nessy', continued in use in parts of northern England into recent times.

Out of Winster extra horses were again permitted on Winster West

153

Bank leading to the Miners' Standard Inn; their 'Standard' was the dish in which they measured lead ore. From this inn the turnpike ran reasonably level past Pikehall, with its tollgate, to Newhaven, where it achieved its object in linking Nottingham with the turnpike to Manchester. In June 1815 'a new fast chariot' was being advertised as a daily service along this road between Matlock and Newhaven and on to Buxton, returning the same evening. Turnpikes converged on Newhaven from five directions and fairs were held there in September and October 'for shows, ribands, toys &c, commonly called a holiday or gig fair'. These fairs were still being held until about 1922.

An unusual feature of this Nottingham-Newhaven turnpike is that in its later years the final three miles to Newhaven were managed by the Cromford to Grangemill to Newhaven Trust, which had been set up in 1804. This Trust took over the Via Gellia (A5012), a road made by Philip Gell, of Hopton Hall, in 1791-2; his purpose was to facilitate transport between his lead mines and the smelting house and canal at Cromford. The 1804 Act authorized the turnpiking of this way out of Cromford to join the Nottingham-Newhaven turnpike at 206593, near Mouldridge Grange; the same Act authorized the Wirksworth-Middleton-Hopton Wood turnpike, and at their junction (262564) a tollhouse was erected. There was also a tollgate as one turned west from Cromford market place; the Nottingham-Newhaven Trust had a gate at Pikehall and, subsequently, the Fenny Bentley to Haddon Trust put a tollgate at Grangemill (p180). An interesting detail is the weathered milestone (183595) west of Pikehall, which appears to read: London 157, To Nottm 33. It is seven miles from the Snitterton milestone (Nottm 26), but the latter is marked 'London 159'. Where along the way has the distance to London been shorn of five miles? The answer would seem to be that from Snitterton a traveller to London would go through Nottingham whereas

154

from the Pikehall area, after 1804, a traveller could turn down the turnpike to Cromford and proceed to London on a shorter route via Derby.

The Second District of the Nottingham to Newhaven Turnpike Trust linked Oakerthorpe, on the Derby to Chesterfield road, with Ashbourne. This turnpike started at Fourlane Ends (389557). After coaches had paid their tolls at Wingfield Gate, they would cross the River Amber and climb to South Wingfield; the gradient was eased in 1825 by blasting down some of the rock. The Manor Hotel at South Wingfield was a coaching inn — the Horse and Groom. The turnpike proceeded via Parkhead to Crich and descended to cross the River Derwent at Whatstandwell Bridge (331543). This curious name has an interesting history: John de Stepul (a place north of Wirksworth) in 1390 agreed with the Abbot of Darley to build a bridge over the Derwent near to a house belonging to Darley Abbey, and the house was defined as that tenanted by Walter Stonewell; over the years his name was forgotten and became corrupted to Whatstandwell.

From the bridge the turnpike climbed steadily to Wirksworth Moor where five roads meet; the Oakerthorpe to Ashbourne road turned north-west to Steeple Grange. The original 1759 route turned down Stoney Hill to pass through Bolehill before climbing the delightfully named Nan Gell's Hill to Steeple Grange; the hillside between Little Bolehill and Bolehill is very unstable and would seem to have slipped not long after the narrow road through these hamlets had been turnpiked,

80   The Via Gellia in Victorian times; it was here joined by the Wirksworth to Hopton Wood turnpike.

for Burdett's map of 1762-7 clearly shows the turnpike running well above a string of houses marked 'Bull Hill'. How many times the old road has been repaired we do not know, but there was a severe landslip in 1947; although it was made good once more it soon slipped again and would seem now (1979) to have been closed permanently to through traffic. The later road along the crest of the steep hillside is still known as Oakerthorpe Road; the Oakerthorpe-Ashbourne District trustees who made it at some date between 1759 and 1767 were reminded by Parliament, many years later, of their duty to fence the west side 'on the edge of the precipice'.

From Steeple Grange the Ashbourne turnpike crossed the Wirksworth to Cromford road, passed through Middleton Cross and joined the present Wirksworth to Ashbourne road (B5035) at Godfreyhole (271537). There was a tollgate (285555) east of Middleton Cross and the tollhouse with its projecting bay has recently been modernized. There was also a tollgate at Godfreyhole; the tollhouse still stands about 200 yd west of the road junction. The object of the detour round Wirksworth would be to maintain a fairly level course, rather than descend 300 ft into the town with a corresponding climb out again. Moreover, the road descending directly from Wirksworth Moor into Wirksworth was part of the earlier (1756) Duffield-Wirksworth turnpike. On the Alfreton-Ashbourne turnpike many of the original milestones are still standing; there are also two Queen Anne guidestones — one opposite Sycamore Farm (267535), the other opposite White House (234524).

The Third District of the Nottingham to Newhaven Turnpike Trust was officially the Wirksworth Moor to Longstone turnpike; it terminated at Hernstone Lane Head (124788) and linked with the Chapel en le Frith turnpike and another Chesterfield turnpike. The first mile or so, from Wirksworth Moor to Steeple Grange was shared with the Second District but the Third District road then went steeply down to Cromford. The riverside road from Cromford to Matlock Bridge owes its origin to two Nottingham men, Smith and Pennell, who in the eighteenth century purchased the lease of the Old Bath, built a hotel and made roads, north to Matlock Bridge and south to Cromford Bridge under the north side of Scarthin Rock; the cutting through Scarthin Rock, offering a more direct route from Cromford to Matlock Bath, was not blasted out until around 1815.

The road system in 1760 at Matlock Bridge has been depicted by E. Paulson as in Map 48. Just as the Newhaven turnpike climbed out of the valley bottom to Snitterton on the west, so in a similar manner did the original Bakewell turnpike climb from the eastern end of the bridge through Dimple to Hackney. Beyond that village the road from Chesterfield that was turnpiked in 1760 — 'Toadhole Turnpike' —

81   (*left*) Milestone on the Ashbourne-Alfreton turnpike.

82   (*right*) The turnpike road through Scarthin Nick, Cromford, in 1837. (*Engraving by T. Allom*)

came into the valley via Two Dales, which on old maps was 'Toadhole' and where there was a tollgate, a smithy and an inn.

The Bakewell turnpike turned down towards Darley Bridge to what is now a crossroads at Four Lane Ends (272625); the road over the bridge was a Chesterfield turnpike linking with the Nottingham to Newhaven turnpike. The road up the Derwent Valley continued along Church Lane and then climbed behind Stancliffe Hall to Northwood (268645), returning to river level at Rowsley. An old road from Rowsley to Bakewell crossed the Derwent then turned north past the church, climbing some 300 ft into the woods before descending Coombes Lane to come into Bakewell at the east end of the bridge. This old road makes a delightful four mile walk.

From Rowsley Bridge yet another turnpike led to Chesterfield; not far from Little Rowsley there is an attractive tollhouse (264661) sited to control traffic passing along the hillside between Northwood, Tinkersley, Fallinge and Beeley. This road from Rowsley Bridge, the B5057 from Darley Bridge and the A632 from Matlock Bridge each leading from Chesterfield to an important crossing of the Derwent, were all authorized in a single Act of Parliament in 1760. A much earlier Act (1739) had authorized the turnpiking of the packhorse route(p108) from Chesterfield over Brampton East Moor to Bakewell; in the 1760 Act it was stipulated that the new Turnpike Trust operating the three more southerly routes from Chesterfield was not to levy tolls from travellers leaving Chesterfield to follow the older Bakewell turnpike, but the latter soon fell into disuse when the turnpike through Rowsley became available.

83   (*left*) Tollhouse at Little Rowsley on the Chesterfield turnpike.

84   (*right*) Milepost on the Rowsley-Chesterfield turnpike.

    The turnpike between Matlock Bridge and Rowsley was improved in stages. First, in 1791, Herbert Greensmith Beard of Stancliffe Hall arranged with the Turnpike Trust for the cutting of a new road outside the western boundary of his park, followed by closure of the original road which had passed too close to the Hall. Then in 1823, by which time Stancliffe Hall had become the property of Heathcote Heathcote, a new road was made from Darley to link with his predecessor's road below Stancliffe. The present road (A6) from Darley into Matlock was made in 1824 and in the following year the 'Toadhole Turnpike' was linked more directly through Four Lane Ends to Darley Bridge.

    The turnpike from Rowsley to Bakewell was controlled by a tollgate at the western end of the village where, on the north side of the road, there stands a tollhouse with quite elaborate stone window-openings; the door has been moved from its original position between the windows and opening directly onto the road. Perhaps this tollhouse was made to look attractive at the request of the Duke of Rutland at nearby Haddon Hall. This line of turnpike, crossing the River Wye by the old Fillyford Bridge (just north of the present bridge), is shown on Burdett's 1762-7 map. It was, in fact, one of the first alterations resulting from the 1759 Act. Until then the road had kept to the eastern side of the Wye and so had passed very close to Haddon Hall; the Duke of Rutland paid for the new turnpike from Rowsley to Bakewell on condition that it was diverted to the opposite side of the river.

    About a mile north-west of Bakewell, the A6 is joined on the left by Crowhill Lane at a point formerly known as Greenhill Hollow; in 1825 the turnpike was improved 'by lowering the hill north and south of the hollow and filling up Greenhill Hollow to the height of 4 feet'. On the

Ashford side of the hollow there was a tollhouse, but in the earlier days of the turnpike this could be bypassed by following the old Derby Gate (p75). The Commissioners for the Bakewell Enclosure Award gave notice in December 1806 that the old road was to be stopped up; travellers then had no alternative but to go through the tollgate and pay their dues.

Ashford in the Water is a place of bridges and we read that in 1776 'Ashford Bridge is so extremely narrow that it is dangerous for Carriages to pass over the same, and that the Battlements are very frequently knocked off by Carriages'. Dr Thomas Brushfield of Ashford wrote that he had seen as many as eighteen coaches pass through the village in a single day. For its protection from modern traffic, the picturesque Sheepwash Bridge (Fig 6) is now closed to all except pedestrians.

From Ashford the turnpike that we have followed from Wirksworth Moor terminated at Monsal Head. When its continuation to Wardlow Mires was being constructed by the trustees of the Chapel en le Frith turnpike, a prehistoric burial mound near Wardlow village, containing seventeen interments in stone cists, was destroyed. At Wardlow Mires a turnpike from Chesterfield formed a T-junction; this 1759 route from Chesterfield was based on a packhorse way (p108) over the moors via Curbar Gap. On the northern side of the road junction at Wardlow Mires stood a tollhouse, and in 1815 this was kept by a widow who was robbed of the tolls and murdered; the murderer, Anthony Lingard, was caught, hanged, and his body gibbeted on high ground, since known as Gibbet Field, near the scene of his crime.

Wardlow Mires, as we have just noted, was on one of the Chesterfield turnpikes: it is mentioned in a Turnpike Act of 1759:

> For repairing and widening the Road from Chesterfield to the Turnpike road at Hernstone Lane Head; and also the Road branching from the said road upon the East Moor through Baslow and Wardlow to the joining of the said Roads near Wardlow Mires; and also the Road leading from the said Road and Branch from Calver Bridge to Baslow Bridge; and also from the Turnpike Road near Newhaven House to the Turnpike Road near Grindleford Bridge in the county of Derby.

This is confusing but may become clearer after study of the accompanying map.

First, there is the 'Road from Chesterfield to the Turnpike Road at Hernstone Lane Head'; the route was through Old Brampton to Bleak House (302721) where there was a change of direction to Robin Hood and Baslow; the turnpike crossed the old bridge and continued up Wheatlands Lane which, significantly, was once known as Chesterfield Gate, and so through Hassop, Great Longstone and Little Longstone, to Monsal Head. In August 1771 an advertisement appeared in the *Derby*

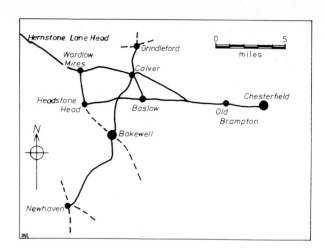

Map 49   The Chester-
field to Hernstone Lane
Head turnpike and
associated turnpikes.

Mercury for the letting of the tolls on the 'Turnpike from Chesterfield to Hernstone Lane Head' at the following gates: Ashgate (347715), Calver, Stoke (240746), Wardlow Mires, Baslow and Conkesbury (210654). The advertising of the tollgates at Wardlow Mires and at Conkesbury, under the heading 'Turnpike from Chesterfield to Hernstone Lane Head' indicates that this was the accepted name of this Turnpike Trust even when referring to one of their branch roads. The Baslow tollgate features in the accounts kept during the building of Hassop church in 1816-18; stone was brought from quarries east of Baslow and the total tolls levied as the stone passed the Baslow gate amounted to a little over £10. The Baslow tollhouse was demolished over a century ago, but one of the windows has been built into a house in Calver; it is inscribed 'Ye Toll House Baslow, Dismantled 1872'. An early nineteenth-century traveller remarked that the tollhouse was 'awkwardly situated at the foot of the bridge' — at its eastern end, almost opposite the watchman's shelter.

In the earliest turnpike days the village of Baslow was clustered around the church and the ancient bridge; this part of Baslow is now known as Bridge End. Nether End, almost half a mile to the east, grew as a result of an exchange of lands between the Duke of Rutland and the Duke of Devonshire in 1823; until then the Nether End area had been Rutland property. The original road leading from Baslow to the junction of the 1803 Owler Bar turnpike with the 1812 Chesterfield turnpike followed the south side of the Bar Brook; when, in 1823, Nether End became Devonshire property, this short length of road was closed and the present line north of the brook was laid out. The Golden Gates leading to Chatsworth House were then erected.

The next road in the 1759 Turnpike Act was 'the Road branching from the said Road upon the East Moor through Baslow and Wardlow to the joining of the said Roads near Wardlow Mires'. If we may insert a comma after 'Wardlow' this means the road from Bleak House on East Moor through Curbar, Calver and Stoney Middleton to Wardlow Mires. The final, steepest, part of the climb to Curbar Gap (now a footpath), was mentioned by Farey in 1817 as not then having been bypassed. The River Derwent was crossed at Calver Bridge, which was washed away in the great flood of August 1799. Near the bridge stood a cotton mill built in 1785-6 on an ideal site with abundant water-power and two turnpikes for transport of the spun yarn — via Chesterfield to Leicester and via Chapel en le Frith to Manchester.

From Calver the road climbed to Stoney Middleton. There is a record of a meeting of the Turnpike Trustees on 2 August 1836 at the Moon Inn, which is still there at Stoney Middleton, to consider the building of a new tollhouse; this was to be almost opposite another inn, the Boot and Shoe. However, although the proposal was adopted, the contract was not signed until 11 November 1840, when William Morton of Froggatt, stonemason, and George Buxton of Stoney Middleton, joiner, contracted to build the tollhouse for £114 14s 0d and to complete the work in two months. The original plan was for a two-storey building, but as it now stands it has one storey only; it is octagonal — designed to match Stoney Middleton's unusual church?

The original road westwards from Stoney Middleton climbed very steeply out of Middleton Dale past Highfields Farm (221752), along Moisty Lane, crossing Dirty Rake into Thunderpit Lane, which was then known as Middleton Road. Water was collected for use at the lead mines in a pool, Holding Dam, at the junction of Moisty Lane and Farnsley Lane, and Nellie Kirkham told of a local tradition that a coach once plunged into the pool and was never seen again! This was evidently a dangerous route and the Petition to Parliament (19 January 1759) recognized this; the intended route was through 'Middleton-dale alias Eyam-

85   Stoney Middleton
tollhouse, built in 1840.

dale'. The turnpike is shown following the dale bottom on Burdett's map of 1767.

The third turnpike referred to in the 1759 Act was the short line from Calver Bridge to Baslow Bridge. Of more interest is the fourth turnpike of this Act, running from Newhaven on the Ashbourne to Buxton turnpike to Grindleford Bridge on the Sheffield turnpike. From Newhaven the first hundred or so yards were shared with the Nottingham turnpike, but the Grindleford road (now A524) then branched off north-east before dipping in and out of Friden Dale. In 1830 the road was improved by making a 9 ft embankment across this dale; the original road can still be seen south of and below the present road. The Trust's surveyor estimated that this improvement would cost £178, but Samuel Dakin and John Taylor contracted to do the work for as little as £98. At the point where the A524 bears right to Youlgreave, the turnpike continued ahead towards Conkesbury. A gatepost built into the wall immediately south of this road junction is an early eighteenth-century guidestone, the four sides reading: 'Yovl[greave], Bvxt[on], [A]shbvrn, Backwel', each followed by 'R' for 'Road'. If this stone is in its original position, a fourth road must have led due west into the lane leading to the Roman road, which in 1700 was still used by travellers to Buxton; alternatively, the route to Buxton could have been along Derby Lane (p67) through Monyash.

Further along this Newhaven to Grindleford turnpike a picnic area (194645) has been made in a disused quarry from which road metal was obtained for the turnpike. Continuing in the same direction an original milestone can be seen on the south of the road (203651) and a more legible one of the same period stands at Conkesbury Farm (210654); the latter milestone is not in its true position, which was at the top of the steep hill on the east side of Conkesbury Bridge. The farm is close to the junction with a lane leading to Youlgreave, and at the south-east corner of this junction there stood a tollhouse; only the garden walls remain. White's *Directory* of 1857 names the tollbar keeper as Edward Bowman, great-grandfather of the late owner of Conkesbury Farm.

After crossing the River Lathkill at Conkesbury Bridge, a steep hill with sharp bends brings the road up to Haddon Fields and so into Bakewell. The Grindleford turnpike then followed the line of the present B6001 through Hassop and Calver; after crossing Stoke Brook, coaches were faced with a formidable climb up Knouchley Hill, which is mentioned by Farey as having a gradient of 1 in 6 and as not having been improved when he was writing in 1817. The Stoke tollhouse stands at the south-east corner of the junction of the turnpike with the road leading down to Froggatt Bridge; there is also a tollhouse at the east end of Grindleford Bridge, where this turnpike from Newhaven terminated.

86 (*top left*) Early eighteenth-century guidestone near Youlgreave.

87 (*bottom left*) Milestone on the Newhaven-Grindleford turnpike.

88 (*below*) Conkesbury Bridge over the River Lathkill.

In 1758 a Turnpike Trust was set up 'to repair and widen the High Road from Barber Fields Cupola to Grindleford Bridge, Great Hucklow, Tideswell, Harding Gate Wall, and Fairfield to Buxton'. This road left Sheffield via Psalter Lane and Banner Cross; the Barber Fields Cupola was at Ringinglow (291837), where there was a tollgate, and from there the road climbed to a height of 1,392 ft on Houndkirk Moor before descending via Fox House Inn through Longshaw Woods to Grindleford. It was not until 1840 that the road down to Grindleford was moved north to its present line, partly at the expense of the Duke of Rutland as the alteration made his Longshaw Lodge more private. This diversion resulted in the awkward road junction at Fox House which, in spite of its signboard showing a fox, is named from the Mr Fox who built it. Tradition has it that Charlotte Brontë had this lonely inn in mind when describing the place where Jane Eyre alighted from a coach on her flight to 'Morton' (Hathersage).

From Grindleford the original Buxton turnpike climbed 500ft in a little over half a mile and then pursued a straight course over Sir William Hill at about 1,400ft. The name Sir William for the hill dates back at least to 1692: Sir William Saville was at that date Lord of the Manor of Eyam, but Sir William Cavendish owned Stoke Hall; the Sir William Hotel was known as the Commercial until about fifty years ago and the Sir William Bagshawe portrayed on the signboard was not born until 1771.

The turnpike continued west through Bretton, then raked down Hucklow Edge to come into Great Hucklow. At Lane Head the Chesterfield to Chapel en le Frith Turnpike was crossed and so Tideswell was reached, where the George Inn was held in high esteem by eighteenth-century travellers; it is still the principal inn but the former extensive stables have been converted to other uses.

Of the next section of this turnpike, Farey, in 1817, wrote:

> The tremendous descents into Monksdale valley and others scarcely less formidable, in the Road between Tideswell and Buxton, might have been avoided and a very good line of Road adopted…by passing through the village of Wheston, by Dale-head and Small-dale, but for the opposition of a Mr. Robert Freeman, who then resided at Wheston, and did not like a Turnpike Road through his village! Egregious folly this, very common in the last age.

A Mr Fairbanks of Sheffield had much to do with the setting out of this 1758 turnpike to Buxton, also the Sheffield to Sparrowpit turnpike; in fact three generations of the Fairbanks family were engaged in road improvements in the Sheffield area. In 1781 they set out new roads from Fox House via Millstone Edge into Hathersage and from Fox House via Froggatt Pole (268790) to Calver, part of the new turnpike from Stoney Middleton via Owler Bar (294780) to Totley. At Owler Bar five roads meet (that from Baslow was turnpiked in 1803) and not surprisingly a tollhouse was erected there; after the gates had been finally thrown open in 1878 the tollboard found its way to Horsleygate (310769) where it was used, face downwards, as a floorboard in a barn.

A major improvement to the Sheffield-Buxton turnpike was effected in 1795 by the abandonment of the exposed Sir William Road and its replacement by a lower route to Tideswell through Eyam and Foolow. The switchback way west of Tideswell remained unaltered yet, travelling along it in 1801, the Rev Richard Warner found the road itself 'hard as adamant and smooth as a bowling green'. It was not until 1812 that the present road down Tideswell Dale into Miller's Dale and up Blackwell Dale was made to link with the 1810 turnpike from Ashford to Buxton

89 Stoke tollhouse between Calver and Grindleford.

90 Barber Fields Cupola tollhouse, Ringinglow near Sheffield

91 Tollhouse at the eastern end of Grindleford Bridge.

92 The George Hotel, Tideswell, with attractive Venetian windows and dating from 1730, was a well-esteemed coaching inn.

93 'The tremendous descents into Monks-dale valley' on the original Buxton-Tideswell turnpike.

via Taddington.

Returning now to the eastern end of the Sheffield–Buxton turnpike, the Houndkirk Moor road remained in use until the Banner Cross to Fox House road was made, at the expense of the Duke of Devonshire, in 1812; it was set out by the Fairbanks family. The road system over the Hallam and Totley Moors was now complete. Two further roads from Owler Bar were projected, one to lead directly to Froggatt Edge, the other to pass through or near Dore to join the Banner Cross turnpike; neither materialized. But in the Derwent Valley a potentially useful turnpike, which became known as Mortimer's Road, had been authorized in 1771 to link Grindleford with Penistone; the route followed the Halifax Gate (p 106) of packhorse days and was intended to permit waggons to take over the transport of wool.

6.5 Cross Country Turnpikes from the West

We have already dealt with turnpikes leading into the Peak District from Manchester and Stockport, but in the reverse direction. Moving south, the next turnpike from the west was that from Macclesfield to Buxton; this road climbs from Cheshire to reach 1,690 ft at the Cat and Fiddle Inn and claims to be the third highest turnpike road in England. Another feature making it of special interest is that the original route as turnpiked in 1759 was superseded in the early nineteenth century along almost its entire length, yet much of the original turnpike is still a metalled road.

As we leave Macclesfield there was a tollgate a short distance beyond the canal, then, a mile out of town, the original turnpike climbed by what is now called Buxton Old Road to pass to the south of Eddisbury Hill. The later turnpike, authorized by Act of Parliament in 1821 and completed by 1823, is now the A537 and this joins the old turnpike at the Setter Dog (956737); as this inn bears the date 1740 it was evidently used by travellers on the old road. There was also a tollgate at this point. For the next half mile the new turnpike coincided with the old, which then kept to the higher ground to a point a little beyond Greenways (975732) but then turned abruptly south, descending to Platting (980724); an earlier hollow-way goes down still more precipitously to Brookhouse (981-728). This loss of height meant a weary pull for the horses as they ascended some 400 ft in the next mile; the later route avoided this detour and loss of height, two miles of new road following more closely the lie of the land. The original turnpike crosses the present main road near Stake; the name suggests that a guidepost once stood there. Nearby was Stonyway Tollgate, this part of the old road then being known as Stonyway. From Stake the original turnpike climbed in a fairly straight line towards the Cat and Fiddle; this half mile is disused and provides a good example of what an early turnpike was like — metalled with small stones and 30 ft wide between low earth banks. Beside it stands an original milestone (Macclesfield 6, London 164) and on this stone J. Thurman, otherwise unknown to history, immortalized himself by carving his name in 1892.

The first turnpike is joined by the later just short of the Cat and Fiddle, but while the later road (A537) bends slightly and passes in front of the inn, the 1759 road maintained a straight course behind the inn, which had not then been built; the overgrown old road between its low earth banks can readily be traced. A traveller on the new turnpike in 1831 described the Cat and Fiddle as 'a newly erected and well accustomed inn or public house'; built by John Ryle, a Macclesfield banker, it must have been a welcome haven for early travellers on these high moors.

The original turnpike descended some 300 ft to the head of Goyt's

94　The earlier (left) and later (right) turnpikes from Macclesfield to Buxton.

95　Stonyway, near the Cat and Fiddle Inn — part of the earlier 1759 turnpike still with its original road surface.

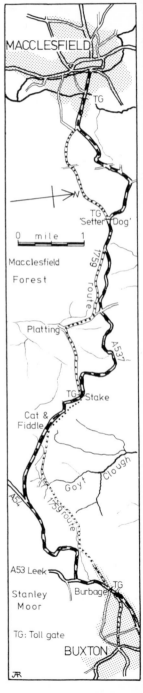

Map 50　The Macclesfield-Buxton turnpike.

96 (*left*) Milestone on the 1759 Macclesfield-Buxton turnpike.

97 (*right*) Iron milepost, cast by J. Harrison of Derby, on the later Macclesfield-Buxton turnpike.

Clough (018716) where there is now a carpark from which the way ahead to Buxton can be followed on foot. This old road, having just lost 300 ft of height by descending into the head of the clough, had to climb out again before beginning its final descent into Buxton; one can appreciate why power was sought in 1821 to construct a new turnpike — at the cost of an extra mile a steady gradient is maintained right from the Cat and Fiddle to Buxton. The old and new roads joined near Burbage Church with a tollgate across the old road. However, whereas the 1759 turnpike terminated at its junction with the Ashbourne road in Higher Buxton, the 1821 turnpike entered Buxton on the north, by what is now St John's Road but was then called Macclesfield New Road; the original turnpike, from the fork near Burbage Church, is still called Macclesfield Old Road. When the new road had been completed in 1823 the old toll-house at Gosling Bar was sold for £45 to the School Trustees of Buxton as it adjoined some of their land; a tollgate at this point (034722) is shown on Burdett's map.

About 1½ miles east of the Cat and Fiddle, the A537 is joined by the A54 from Congleton. Leaving Congleton via Buglawton, this turnpike bridged the canal and then turned abruptly north at Fingerpost House; after recrossing the canal and then the River Dane at Colley Mill, the road turned east to cross the Sandon to Bullock Smithy Turnpike at Smithy Green. From there the road climbs to Cleulow Cross with grand views marred only by the incongruous Post Office Tower. It would seem that in turnpike days Cleulow Cross had another name, for when the Rev John Skinner travelled through Congleton to Buxton in January 1803, he recorded that 'from Cross-of-the-Moor the most dreary road imaginable conducted us into Buxton'. Between the Cross and Buxton he would have had to pass through one tollgate at Allgreave (974669), another at Dane Head (008698) and a third, Axe Edge Tollgate, three miles short of Buxton near Boothman's Cottages (027714).

Before we leave this area mention must be made of a plan dated 1813 for a 'Turnpike Road leading from Flash Toll Gate to Black Clough . . . to join the Turnpike Road leading from Congleton to Buxton near Dane Head Coal Pits'. This turnpike never materialized but the plan (now in the Cheshire Record Office) shows a route that can still readily be followed, first as a metalled lane branching from the Leek-Buxton road past Oxensitch to Readyleech Green (022686), dwindling eventually into a track that, in Black Clough, crosses from Staffordshire into Derbyshire, and then into Cheshire. Tollgates already existed at each end of this proposed road so the promoters could scarcely have expected to levy still further tolls along its short length. There were many coal pits in the area, also the important Reeve Edge Quarries; the pits, quarry and road were all on land owned either by the Duke of Devonshire or by the Earl of Derby. There was already a track (Yates's map of 1775) and one can only assume that the proposal to develop it into a turnpike was for the benefit of the pits and quarries, with consequent increases in royalties for the two landowners.

Early nineteenth-century travellers from Macclesfield or Congleton after they had taken refreshment at Buxton, could turn north along the new linkroad to Barmoor Clough (077795), constructed by the Trustees of the Buxton to Manchester Turnpike as authorized by an Act of 1801; this provided a gently graded route to Chapel en le Frith. The old road turned more to the west at Dove Holes, passing over Martinside, and this climb necessitated a very steep descent to Chapel en le Frith. This old road is still called Ashbourne Lane, leading south from Chapel through Buxton to Ashbourne. North of Chapel en le Frith the road to Hayfield and Glossop was turnpiked in 1792; at Chapel Milton, where this

98 Tollhouse at Hayfield on the Chapel en le Frith to Glossop turnpike.

turnpike turned off the road to Chinley, there is a house (052824) named Tollbar View bearing the date 1878. Hayfield was a stage out of Buxton and horses were changed at the George Inn, which claims to have a history going back to 1575.

Those travelling from Buxton eastwards to Bakewell prior to 1810 had to follow the Ashbourne turnpike as far as Brierlow Bar; there they would turn onto a parish road to Chelmorton where, for part of his salary, the schoolmaster depended on the interest on £101 secured on the Buxton turnpike and £200 secured on the Cheadle turnpike from Brierlow Bar — the former yielding 5 per cent but paid infrequently, the latter yielding only 3½ per cent but paid as and when due. From Chelmorton further parish roads led through Sheldon to Ashford.

It had long been realized that to follow the River Wye from Buxton to Bakewell would provide an almost level road, very different from that through Chelmorton. In 1784, for example, a Dr Pearson suggested that 'with no great labour a path might be made for two horses to travel abreast' from Buxton alongside the Wye in Ashwood Dale, adding 'A work of this kind has been in contemplation, but is not likely to be soon executed'. It would seem, however, that the fifth Duke of Devonshire did make a carriage-road for some way along Ashwood Dale; carriages could return to Buxton along the Duke's Drive to Sherbrook laid out in 1795. But those who have walked down the valley beyond Ashwood Dale and through Chee Dale, particularly if the river happened to be high, will know that this was no way for a turnpike. Yet, at the height of the coaching era, in 1828, a plan was prepared by one of the Fairbanks surveyors for a road to be known as the Monsal Dale to Barmoor Turnpike; the plan shows it following the Wye through Monsal Dale, Miller's Dale and Chee Dale, turning then up Great Rocks Dale with a short link into Ashwood Dale through which, by that date, a turnpike had, in fact been made.

This Buxton-Ashford turnpike was authorized by an Act passed on 1 June 1810. Construction work along Ashwood Dale involved some channeling of the River Wye and the blasting down of the original Lover's Leap. The most spectacular feature of the new turnpike was the steadily graded shelf cut into the limestone cliff of Topley Pike. A traveller in 1811 declared that 'the prospect it affords...is terrific and sublime; above the traveller beholds a shattered, overhanging rock, apparently ready at every moment to overwhelm him; below, a rapid river, foaming against the falling fragments, washes the feet of the steep on which he journeys.' Even twenty-five years later the Topley Pike road was still held in awe: 'The piled and laden coaches which we see every evening safely rattling into the White Lion in Nottingham, have all weathered this fearful ascent; and everyone that sets out in the morning for Manchester has to trot, gallop, slip, slidder, scratch or tumble down it!'

However, the merits of this new turnpike were quickly recognized by the Trustees of the notoriously ill-routed Buxton-Grindleford turnpike and in 1812 they constructed, with a member of the Fairbanks family as surveyor, a linking road from Tideswell into Miller's Dale and up Blackwell Dale; tolls were taken at a gate on the south of the river in Miller's Dale, thus catching traffic using Long Lane to or from Tadding-ton. The Buxton-Ashford turnpike passed down Taddington's long street, at the side of which stands a cast-iron milepost of economical design: the word 'London', because it was to appear at the top of every milepost along the turnpike, was cast embossed, but the actual distances and the other place names were painted on. Taddington is now bypassed via a dual carriageway, which is rejoined by the turnpike before the descent through Taddington Dale, the turnpike ending, as it began, alongside the River Wye into Ashford. Arrived there, it is worth pausing to watch the lorries pound along what is now Trunk Road A6 and to remember that they are following a turnpike that was so well engineered in 1810 that, even today, there is little scope for its improve-ment.

Londoners travelling to Buxton to take the waters soon discovered this scenic route, following first the Derwent through Matlock then the Wye through Bakewell; Spring Gardens, into which the new turnpike led, displaced Upper Buxton as the fashionable shopping centre.

Referring to the further end of this turnpike, Farey, who had col-lected most of the information for his survey of Derbyshire several years before it was actually published (1817), mentioned that the Buxton-Ashford turnpike was 'now completed, I believe', and continued:

From Ashford, this new line is continued forwards by a private road across Birchill's Farm, to join and cross the Bakewell and Baslow Road, and thence by a new public Road, through Pilsbury [Pilsley] to Edensor Inn near to Chatsworth House; whence there is a private Road through the Park to Chatsworth Lower Bridge, and thence a Parish Road in pretty good repair completes this line to Great Rowsley Bridge.

Farey's information, as usual, was correct. The 'private road across Birchill's Farm' was made at the expense of the Duke of Devonshire; not surprisingly, work began at Edensor and 3½ of the 4 miles of new road required to reach Ashford and join the new turnpike to Buxton, had been made when, in 1812, the whole length was taken over as a turnpike and completed. The tollhouse erected at Rowdale (214709) still stands, a symbolic gate and bell added to its gable. This short turnpike terminated at the Edensor Inn, the handsome building set back to the east of the road. South from Edensor, the road passing through Chatsworth Park to the

99   Iron milepost on the Ashford-Edensor road which was begun by the Duke of Devonshire as a private road but then completed (in 1812) as a turnpike. These mileposts, like those on the Ashford-Buxton road, have only 'London' cast on them — the other place names were painted on.

crossing of what Farey called 'Chatsworth Lower Bridge', remained private; it was laid out during the period when Capability Brown was advising the Fourth Duke on landscaping — and how fine a road we now have! The last link, from the crossing of the Derwent to the turnpike at Rowsley, remained the parish road that Farey had found 'in pretty good repair'.

Returning to the western boundary of the Peak Park, the next major point of entry, still working south, is Leek. In 1765 Parliament authorized the turnpiking of the road from Newcastle under Lyme through Leek to Longnor and Hassop, together with a 'Branch from Middlehills to join the Macclesfield Turnpike Road near Buxton'. Middlehills is the area of moorland around the Royal Cottage (026640), near to which the Longnor road bears east from the present A53; the 'Branch from Middlehills' was the continuation of the Leek turnpike from the Royal Cottage to its junction with the Macclesfield turnpike (A54) at Ladmanlow (042720). This 'Branch road' leading to Buxton is now the more important, but the chief purpose of the 1765 Turnpike Act was evidently to link Newcastle under Lyme with Hassop and the Chesterfield turnpike; we will consider the reason for this later, but will first follow the pre-turnpike route from Leek to Buxton.

The only villages lying between Leek and Buxton are Meerbrook and Flash; neither is on the present Leek to Buxton road, which, except for comparatively recent improvements at Upper Hulme and Cistern's Clough, is identical with the turnpike road. We have seen how the older roads near Matlock Bridge passed through the neighbouring villages: Bradnop, near Leek, also stood on a pre-turnpike highway. That the same is true of Meerbrook and Flash is confirmed by the map of Staffordshire made by Emanuel Bowen; this map was first printed in 1749 and was re-issued at various dates between 1760 and 1800 in successive editions of *The Large English Atlas* by Bowen and Kitchin. However, the 1749 map remained unaltered except for the imprint at its foot, so we may safely take Bowen's line of road from Leek to Buxton as that in use in 1749, some sixteen years before the Turnpike Trust began work on its new line of turnpike.

Bowen's pre-turnpike road passed through both Meerbrook and Flash. It set out from Leek past 'Dela Cress' — the old abbey of Dieu la Cresse — to Meerbrook; the next place marked is 'Winyates', now Windygates (004618), a farm bearing the date 1634 and the ancient home of the Broughs. The way then climbed through the gap in the Roaches between Five Clouds and Hen Cloud; it can be seen as a hollow-way curving up from Windygates. The next place name on Bowen's map is 'Goldsich'; on the modern map we find both Goldsitch House and Goldsitch Moss lying on a fairly direct line to Flash. The old way seems to have passed north-west of Ann Roach, for hollow-ways descend from that area to Flash Bottom (022661); from there it may have reached Flash by way of Wilson Knowl. No further place names appear on Bowen's map, the road merely continuing across the county boundary in the direction of Buxton. A packhorse way continues north between Oliver Hill (1,684ft and the highest hill in Staffordshire) and Wolf Edge to Hilltop (028683), then passing west of Axe Edge. The way is followed by a footpath to Five Stones (028694), a prominent outcrop landmark, and Dane Head; from there the way would lead into the old road from Macclesfield to Buxton. However, the original (1765) turnpike seems to have been on the east side of Axe Edge, turning round the head of the River Manifold to follow what is now a byroad past Gamballs Green (036679), descending to cross the infant Dove only to ascend again to Cistern's Clough (035698). This route is shown on Burdett's map and is accepted by Radley and Penny as the original line of the turnpike; it involved steep hills and was probably based on a pre-existing packhorse way. The Turnpike Trustees would soon realize the advantage of cutting a new road on a steady gradient along the flank of Axe Edge — the excellent road we have today.

We will now propose an answer to the question — why, in 1765, should Parliamentary sanction have been sought for the turnpiking of a road from Newcastle under Lyme to Hassop along an old way that had 'become very deep and ruinous, and in many Places goes over Morasses, Boggs and Mountains, and is very narrow and incommodious'. One may assume that those promoting the Bill hoped for some benefit. The promoters and subsequent Turnpike Trustees included some of the most prosperous of the North Staffordshire master-potters, and if we couple this with the nature of the goods carried along this route in the eighteenth century, the reason for making a turnpike over so many miles of thinly populated moorland becomes plain. *The Day to Day Accounts of Robert Thornhill (1740-1820) of Great Longstone* record that a carrier named John Hayne of Hardings Booth, near Longnor, transported some hundreds of tons of chert from the Great Longstone area through Monyash and Longnor to the North Staffordshire potteries; chert is a very hard form of silica rock and it was used in the form of large blocks for the runners and pavers in the old type of potters' panmills. Josiah Wedgwood and his fellow master-potters needed a good road along which their supply of Derbyshire chert could be transported. Robert Thornhill's eighteenth-century accounts also show that the chert waggons did not return empty; crates of pottery, as well as farm produce from the intervening villages, were brought back, in some cases en route to Sheffield.

In addition to the North Staffordshire potters, the poorer inhabitants of Longnor also benefitted from this turnpike. On the west wall of St Bartholomew's Church there, a list of charities includes a bequest, dated 1793, from John Robinson of the Fawside, near Longnor, of 'the interest of £196 9s 6d secured upon the Leek Turnpike road'. At that period Longnor was a market town and the market hall still overlooks the little square; it is worth more than a passing glance. So, too, is the early eighteenth-century guidestone which stands near the village crossroads. The Crewe and Harpur Hotel was a coaching inn and a guidebook of 1803 states that one of the three coach-routes from London to Buxton at that time was via Lichfield and Longnor; from Lichfield the traveller would proceed through Uttoxeter and Cheadle, from where a series of turnpikes (p177) led through Longnor via Brierlow Bar to Buxton.

The Newcastle to Hassop Turnpike included some long and steep hills, notably that through Upper Hulme (013609), now partly bypassed, and that above Crowdicote (101652). Because of these hills, the Court of Quarter Sessions allowed ten horses for a waggon and five for a cart with wheels of 6in breadth, and five horses for a waggon and five for a cart with wheels less than 6in breadth. At a meeting of the Turnpike Trustees held on 5 June 1781 in Longnor at the Harper Arms Inn (now the Crewe and Harpur), the tollgates at Leek Edge and at Longnor were let to the highest bidder. Fifty years later a notice in the *Staffordshire Advertiser* mentioned Kirkdale tollgate. On the 1840 OS map tollgates are shown along the Newcastle to Hassop turnpike at Leek Edge (998572), where the tollhouse still stands on the north side of the road near the Moss Rose Inn; at Longnor, going up the hill into the village after crossing the River Manifold; Monyash, just before entering the village square; Kirkdale, at the junction with the Sheldon road (182687). However, when notice was

100 Horse Lane, Monyash. Originally on a packhorse route to Ashford, it later became part of the Newcastle under Lyme to Hassop turnpike.

101 Ipstones tollhouse on the Cheadle to Butterton Moor End turnpike.

given that the tollgates along this road would finally be thrown open on 1 November 1873, mention was also made of a gate at Crowdicote; the tollhouse there is now a neat cottage down the road from the Packhorse Inn, with a small side-window facing up the road. This same notice also referred to the throwing open of the tollgate at Ladmanlow (042720) on the branch turnpike from the Royal Cottage to Buxton; this turnpike entered Buxton by way of Green Lane, in former days more commonly known as Leek Road. There was a tollgate at Green Lane (near the Burbage traffic lights) and this gate and the Ladmanlow gate were frequently auctioned together; in 1794 they had been let to a toll-collector for £319, a sum indicative of very considerable traffic. The Ladmanlow gate controlled both the Leek road and the short turnpike, authorized in

1773, linking that road with the Ashbourne turnpike at Brierlow Bar.

Four miles south-east of Leek, at Bottom House, the Leek to Ashbourne turnpike is crossed by the Cheadle to Butterton Moor End turnpike, which was authorized in 1770. From Bottom House this cross-country turnpike climbs over the southern end of Morridge at a height of 1,211 ft, and this provides a fine point of entry to the western side of the Peak Park, with long views over the Hamps Valley. From the viewpoint the road descends to Onecote, where there was a tollgate. The old way from Onecote to Butterton was up Titterton Lane, which branches to the south of the present road (B5053) just beyond Onecote Old Hall; however, when Yates made his survey for his 1775 map, Titterton Lane had already been superseded by the present line of road. Almost opposite to the junction of Titterton Lane with the new road, a track leads to Butterton Moor End Farm, and from the location of this farm one would deduce that the Cheadle to Butterton Moor End turnpike originally terminated at the bottom of Titterton Lane. The continuation of the road north-east from Butterton Moor End was sometimes referred to in toll-letting advertisements as the Onecote to Newhaven Turnpike, but in the *Derby Mercury* for 25 May 1781, there appeared the following notice:

> Toll-gates on the Turnpike Road leading from Butterton Moor End... to the Three Mile Stone in the Turnpike Road leading from Buxton to Ashbourne; and from Blacton Moor, in the County of Stafford, to... near Newhaven; and from Warslow to Ecton Mine... known as Brownloe Bar, Glutton Bar, Holme End Bar, Dale Bar and Hartington Mill Bar... to be let at the *Horse and Trumpet* in Hartington, 28th June 1781.

Brownlow Bar was a little to the north-east of Brownlow Bridge (074576) but no trace of the tollhouse remains. A couple of hundred yards up the present road to Warslow there is a lane on the left to Elkstone and close to its junction with the main road a stile gives access to a footpath leading north; this path is on the line of the turnpike referred to in the 1781 advertisement. In about half a mile, the footpath comes between walls and is in places metalled with small stones. When it reaches Blacton Moor (077589), the turnpike leading north kept straight ahead to pass over the eastern shoulder of Revidge and then over Reapsmoor to Longnor where, in 1840, there was a tollgate at the junction with the lane leading into the road to the Royal Cottage. Beyond Longnor, there was another tollgate near Glutton (085671) and the turnpike terminated at Brierlow Bar on the present A515.

The Newhaven branch turned east from Blacton Moor past Water Gap Farm (once an inn) and into Warslow. This was still the principal road into Warslow when the first OS map was issued in 1840. The branch turnpike from Warslow to Ecton, with Dale Tollbar across its upper end, was for traffic to and from the Ecton copper mines. The old way from Warslow to Hulme End followed the pleasant lane leading to Cowlow (100593); Hulme End Bar stood immediately east of the bridge over the River Manifold, and Hartington Mill Bar was across the turnpike (Mill Lane) just west of where it is joined by the overgrown lane leading in from Crossland Sides. The short turnpike from Hartington Mill to Newhaven was authorized in the same year (1770) as the road leading into it from Warslow; it provided the final link in a cross country line of turnpikes from Cheadle to Chesterfield or Sheffield.

The Onecote to Newhaven turnpike makes a good route from the west to Hartington and Beresford Dale; an equally attractive way to the southern end of Dovedale is provided by the Blythe Marsh to Thorpe turnpike, which was authorized in 1762 by the same Act of Parliament that sanctioned the turnpiking of the Ashbourne to Leek road. Blythe Marsh lies at the southern extremity of the Stoke on Trent conurbation, on the Derby-Uttoxeter-Newcastle turnpike, which had been authorized in 1759; the cross country road from Blythe Marsh to Thorpe therefore linked two major turnpikes leading from Derby to the north-west. The route lay through Cheadle, where a toll house still stands on the south side of the road entering the town. The original way from Cheadle to Oakamoor passed through the yard of Highshutt Farm (031-437), down the fields to Old Furnace (041436), and then down Stony Dale; one of the first improvements made by the Turnpike Trustees in 1762 was to cut a new road linking Cheadle and Oakamoor along the line now used. At Oakamoor there was a tollhouse east of the Cricketers Arms, just beyond the byroad leading to Whiston. The pre-turnpike track east from Oakamoor can be followed as a footpath past Goldenhill Farm to the Old Star; this house, once a roadside inn, lies a quarter of a mile south of the present Star Inn (065456).

The Blythe Marsh to Thorpe turnpike joins the A52 near Ruehill tollhouse, which stands on the north side of the road by a lane leading to Caldon Grange; a further mile brings us to Stanton Dale tollhouse (109-477), rebuilt in 1845 but retaining some of the original windows. The Leek to Ashbourne turnpike is crossed at Calton Moor; in coaching days the farm west of the crossroads was an inn — the Red Lion. The Blythe Marsh to Thorpe turnpike continued north-east, passing below the hill-top plantation known as Hazleton Clump and offering a fine view of the hills around Dovedale; if that is our destination we must leave the turnpike at Blore cross roads, turning left for Ilam and the famous Stepping Stones below Thorpe Cloud. The turnpike continued east at Blore crossroads, where there was a tollhouse, passing close to Coldwall Farm and crossing the River Dove by Coldwall Bridge; near the bridge there is a milestone — Cheadle 11 — in the position where it was set up in 1822.

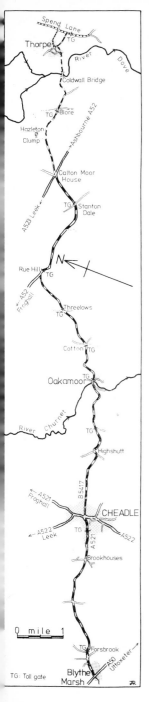

102 (*top*) Oakamoor tollhouse on the Blythe Marsh to Thorpe turnpike, early this century.

103 Coldwall Bridge on the Blythe Marsh to Thorpe turnpike.

104 (*right*) Milestone near Coldwall Bridge set up in 1822.

Map 51 The Blythe Marsh to Thorpe turnpike.

Thorpe village was entered near the Norman church. When the Turnpike Trust was formed in 1762, the route was the overgrown track east of the church leading into the lane that passes Broadlowash Farm to join the old Ashbourne to Buxton turnpike, Spend Lane, near a tollhouse (163501); a new road was made in 1765 passing west of Thorpe church to meet the old Ashbourne road at the Dog and Partridge.

Our survey of the major turnpikes of the Peak District is now nearly complete, the only remaining gateway from the west being Ashbourne. We have already dealt with the Ashbourne to Wirksworth and Ashbourne to Buxton turnpikes, but two miles north of Ashbourne a turnpike was authorized in 1811 to lead from the Buxton road via Grangemill to Haddon; this road is now the B5056. As far as Grangemill this road did not exist when Burdett surveyed Derbyshire in the years 1762-67, but from Grangemill to Alport travellers could at that time still follow the Old Portway as they had done for centuries. A detailed strip-map dated 1807 exists showing how the turnpike was to be set out. Tollhouses were erected at Hipley, where Pasture Lane descends from Brassington, and at Grangemill. The Hipley tollhouse was still inhabited in the early 1960s but has since been demolished; the Grangemill tollhouse, much altered, is now used as a farm building. Towards the northern end of this turnpike a tollgate (231644) was erected at the junction of a lane to Stanton-in-Peak and the wood on the hillside became known as Tolls Wood. The turnpike terminated at Picory Corner (239658) where it joined the Rowsley to Bakewell road. The Fenny Bentley to Haddon turnpike,

105   Milestone on the Ashbourne-Haddon turnpike (now B5056) authorised in 1811.

180

which now carries so much quarry traffic, was not profitable to those who paid for its construction. By 1865 the Trustees were £14,908 in debt; the many creditors included the Duke of Rutland (£900), the Duke of Devonshire (£500), and the Gell family (£500). Although by that date the Trustees could have had little hope of making good their losses, they promoted a further Act of Parliament to permit them to carry on for an additional fifteen years during which time they would devote the toll receipts to: (1) paying for the promotion of the Act; (2) paying the tollhouse keepers and maintaining the gates; (3) paying 1 per cent interest to their creditors; (4) maintaining the road to the extent of £75 a year; (5) repaying borrowed capital; (6) additional work on the road. With maintenance cut to the bone, what is now a pleasant and well-engineered route from Ashbourne to Haddon Hall or Chatsworth House became a deteriorating turnpike until, in 1881-2, Parliament sanctioned the winding-up of this Turnpike Trust and the tollgates were thrown open.

Finally we have the turnpike from Ashbourne to Belper authorized in 1764; the actual terminus was a mile or so east of Belper at Openwoodgate, where it joined the Derby to Sheffield turnpike. The first point of interest on leaving Ashbourne was the Machine Inn, now derelict. Until about sixty-five years ago the cottage west of the inn had a weighbridge in front of it; against the east wall there was a smithy. In turnpike days a waggon could be weighed while one of the horses had a shoe replaced; but before the waggoner went next door for a pot of ale he would anxiously watch the weighing — an Act of Parliament of 1741 had authorized turnpike trustees to erect weighing machines and impose an additional toll of 20s per cwt on any laden waggon weighing more than three tons.

Along the road the normal tolls were taken at Sturston Gate, a mile out of town; this tollgate is mentioned in the *Derby Mercury* for the 19 January 1781, where it is stated that the total tolls collected there during the previous year amounted to £82. Sturston Tollhouse has been untenanted for some years; its demolition would rob this road of some of its history, but should this unhappily occur the site would still be remembered as Tollgate Farm stands opposite. There were other gates along this road at Shottle and at Belper Bridge.

Between Shottlegate and Belper, at Blackbrook, the turnpike along which lorries now thunder, is crossed by the prehistoric Portway and by the Longwalls Roman Road. Where better to end a journey through history than at this point where so many centuries of travel intersect.

Bibliography

Abbreviations

DAJ   *Derbyshire Archaeological Journal*
DC   *Derbyshire Countryside*
DM   *Derbyshire Miscellany*

General

Cameron, K. *The Place-names of Derbyshire* (Cambridge 1959)
Dodgson, J.McN. *The Place-names of Cheshire* (Cambridge 1970-2)
Jervoise, E. *The Ancient Bridges of Mid and Eastern England* (1932)

Chapter 1 Prehistoric Trackways

Cockerton, R.W.P. 'The Portway, Castlegate, Derby Gate and Doctor's Gate', DC, **2** (1932), 25, 54, 83; **3** (1933), 39, 60, 86
Preston, F.L. 'The Hill Forts of the Peak', DAJ, **74** (1954), 1

Chapter 2 Roman Roads

Cockerton, R.W.P. 'The Doctor's Gate', DC, **3** (1933), 19, 39
Cockerton, R.W.P. 'On the Development of the Roman Street System with Special Reference to Derbyshire', DAJ, **73** (1953), 67
Cockerton, R.W.P. 'The Hereward Street', DAJ, **80** (1960), 71
Lomas, J. 'Problems of the Roman Road between Buxton and Little Chester', DAJ, **78** (1958), 103
Margary, I.D. *Roman Roads in Britain* (1967)
Preston, F.L. 'The Roman East-West Road through Sheffield', *Yorks Archaeolog J*, 39 (1957), 329
Smithard, W. 'The Roman Road between Little Chester and Minninglow', DAJ, **32** (1910), 125
Smithard, W. 'Notes on the Roman Roads called Batham Gate and Doctor Gate', DAJ, **33** (1911), 95
Wroe, P., and Mellor, P. 'A Roman Road between Buxton and Melandra Castle', DAJ, **91** (1971), 40. See also their notes in *Britannia*, **6** (1975), 242, 244; **7** (1976), 321; **8** (1977), 388; **9** (1978), 430.

Chapter 3 Dark and Middle Ages

Cockerton, R.W.P. 'The Portway, Castlegate and Doctor's Gate', DC, **2** (1932), 25, 54, 83; **3** (1933), 39, 60, 86
Jusserand, J.J. *English Wayfaring Life in the Middle Ages* (1961)
Kirkham, Nellie. 'Ancient Boundaries', DM, **5** (1970), 136; **6** (1971), 5, 35

Chapter 4 Tudor and Stuart Period

Fiennes, C. *Journeys* (Ed by C.Morris, 1947)
Ogilby, J. *Itinerarium Angliae* (1675)

Chapter 5 Packhorse Ways and Drovers' Roads

Bonser,K.J. *The Drovers* (1970)
Crump, W.B. 'Saltways from the Cheshire Wiches', *Trans Lancs Cheshire Antiq Soc,* **54** (1939), 84
Radley, J. 'Peak District Roads Prior to the Turnpike Era', *DAJ,* **83** (1963), 39

Chapter 6 Turnpike Era

Brighouse, W.H. 'In the Steps of a Turnpike', *Derbyshire Life,* **32** no 3 (1967), 21; no 8, 26
Copeland, J. *Roads and their Traffic, 1750-1850* (1968)
Defoe, D. *A Tour thro' the Island of Great Britain* (1724-6)
Dodd, A.E. and Dodd, E.M. 'The Old Road from Ashbourne to Leek', *Trans N Staffs Field Club,* **83** (1948-9), 29; **84** (1949-50), 46
Dodd, E.M. 'The Blythe Marsh to Thorpe Turnpike', *N Staffs J Field Studies,* **5** (1965), 1
Farey, J. *General View of the Agriculture of Derbyshire,* **3** (1817)
Hayhurst, R. 'Notes on Toll Houses', *DM,* **5** no 1 (1969), 49
Heath, J.E. 'Stage Coach Routes in 18th and 19th Century Derbyshire', *DM,* **5** no 3 (1970), 172
Johnson, R. 'The Nottingham-Newhaven Turnpike Road', *DM,* **5** no 1 (1969), 5
Lysons, D., and Lysons, S. *Magna Britannia,* 5 (1817)
Paulson, E. 'Road Development in Darley and Matlock', *DM,* **5** no 1 (1969), 38
Radley, J., and Penny, S.R. 'The Turnpike Roads of the Peak District', *DAJ,* **92** (1972), 93
Thornhill, R. 'Notes on some Derbyshire Toll-houses and Turnpike Roads', *DM* **4** no 4 (1968), 185
Thornhill, R. 'Turnpike Roads', *DM,* **5** no 4 (1970), 198
Twells, H.S. 'The Beginning of a Turnpike Trust', *DAJ,* **66** (1946), 24

Acknowledgements

We remain indebted to those mentioned in the Acknowledgements in the First Edition, and further help has been received from several people there recorded, especially from Miss J.C.Sinar (County Archivist, Matlock) and from I.E.Burton (Buxton Library); J.A.Robey has kindly prepared several additional maps and J.S.Plant has placed us further in his debt by providing more photographs.

In our revision of the chapter on Roman Roads we have been given valuable assistance by P.M.Jennings (Ashbourne); we also gladly acknowledge help from P.Wroe and P.Mellor, whose field-work in recent years has added considerably to our knowledge of the precise lines of several Roman Roads in the area.

During our revision of the chapter on the Turnpike Era we have received much help from S.R.Penny (Sheffield), who has taken endless trouble in the checking of the dates of Turnpike Acts; we have also made extensive use of the article on the Peak District turnpikes jointly written by him and the late J.Radley.

Assistance in resolving various other details has been freely given by: B.C.Redwood and Mrs H.Chambers (Cheshire Record Office), R.G.Hughes (Derby Museum), D.Hey (Sheffield University), J.Scott (Glossop Historical Society), W.Shimwell (Youlgreave), N.A.Keen (Lea, near Matlock) and J.N.Wordingham (Taddington).

Since publication of the First Edition, we have been able to carry out much additional field-work in the course of which we have invariably met with courtesy and kindness during impromptu conversations by the wayside. To those who have patiently listened to our questions and have then shared their local knowledge, we offer sincere thanks; chance encounters have often provided information that would otherwise not have come to our notice and might never have been recorded.

The illustrations used have been provided by the following:
BBC Hulton Picture Library: 73-4, 80; G.E.Ellis: 45; Derbyshire Record Office: 58-9; A.E.Dodd: 1, 3, 13, 29, 31, 40-1, 57, 62, 68-9; A.Goldstraw: 33, 54; Pickfords Ltd 30, 60; J.S.Plant: 8, 11, 15, 16, 18, 21-2, 32, 35, 43-4, 46, 48-9, 61, 67, 77-8, 86, 91, 93, 98; C.L.M.Porter: 38-9; J.A.Robey: 2, 4-5, 7, 19, 20, 23-8, 34, 36-7, 47, 50-1, 53, 56, 63-5, 70-2, 79, 81, 83-5, 87-9, 92, 94-7, 99-101, 103-5; Sheffield Newspapers Ltd: 75-6, 90; B.Spencer: 6; P.L.Wilson: 102.

Index